Bonnie
Hyson

STEVE 253-230-7497

STARVE A BULLY,
FEED A CHAMPION

Also by Jacob Glass

Invocations: Calling Forth the Light That Heals
The Crabby Angels Chronicles

STARVE A BULLY, FEED A CHAMPION

101 Days of Spiritual Boot Camp for
Attaining Serenity, Confidence, Mental Discipline
& Joy in a World Gone Mad.

> You don't live the life you deserve.
> You live the life you think you deserve.

Jacob Glass

BALBOA.
PRESS
A DIVISION OF HAY HOUSE

Balboa Press books may be ordered through booksellers or by contacting:

Balboa Press
A Division of Hay House
1663 Liberty Drive
Bloomington, IN 47403
www.balboapress.com
1-(877) 407-4847

ISBN: 978-1-4525-5234-7 (sc)
ISBN: 978-1-4525-5233-0 (hc)
ISBN: 978-1-4525-5232-3 (e)

Library of Congress Control Number: 2012908968

Printed in the United States of America

Balboa Press rev. date: 05/24/2012

Dedication

*For these precious three: Bill Thetford, Zan Gaudioso & Kaytra
Parkman*

Epigraph

To heal is to make happy.
A Course in Miracles

Table of Contents

Preface

The truth about you is so lofty that nothing unworthy of God is worthy of you.

                                        -A Course in Miracles

You were not born to merely be a survivor. You were born to be a THRIVER because you are a born champion! Saying you are a survivor is more than obvious. Every single living person on the planet is a survivor. If you didn't die, you're a survivor. Even if you are incapacitated in a bed hooked up to machines, you're still a survivor. You made it this far and survived whatever mild to devastating problems and challenges you've had thus far—so congratulations. But no matter how devastating and destructive your past may have been, and no matter how "damaged" you may think you are, and even if you feel there is not another living person on the planet who truly sees your value and worth, it does not change the fact that you were spiritually coded to thrive, flourish, prosper and grow in the Light. There is no need to justify the space you occupy through your hard work and struggles. One of the Master Teachers came to tell us that we may have life, and have it more ABUNDANTLY.

Whether you've survived cancer, drug addiction, rape, incest, poverty, divorce, AIDS, a heart attack, financial ruin, bullying, crippling self-doubt, physical violence, abandonment, the death of a child, public humiliation, betrayal, the loss of your reputation, imprisonment, chronic illness and pain, scandal or any number of ways that life can seem to take you down, the fact is you are still here, and that is a very good thing. I honor you and your path. I acknowledge you for making it through whatever obstacles and challenges you've faced in your life and am so happy you made it to this point. But to continue to declare yourself as a survivor is to give your subconscious mind the message to look for, focus on and even create situations and catastrophes to conquer. You are not a conqueror but rather a champion! You see your self-perception will greatly influence the life that your subconscious mind will create for you. You see, you are who YOU say you are. You will act like whoever you believe yourself to be. To change your life, you must change your self-perception. No matter what anyone else is saying about you, YOU are the final authority on who you really are. YOU are the one who must see your value and worth no matter what!

You CAN go from being a survivor to being a THRIVER and a true champion more quickly than you may realize. And it all begins with YOU, right now, this very moment. It begins WITHIN YOU as you begin to think different thoughts and choose different feelings. It will take willingness, consistency and tremendous dedication. You will need to unlearn old habits of thinking, speaking and behaving and develop new ones. You will need to LET GO of what doesn't work in order to take hold of what does. You will be required to turn away from the voices of the world, which seek to tear you down and instead turn to a Voice within your own sanctuary within. Essentially, it will be necessary to let go of being right in order to be happy, peaceful, joyous and free.

Acknowledgments

I want to take this opportunity to thank my wonderful student practitioners for their support and their tremendous willingness in doing the daily work which leads to JOY. And also big thanks to the Miracle Distribution Center, Marianne Williamson and her team, Byron Katie, the fabulous RuPaul, Unity of Santa Barbara, Lori Newman, Inn at the Park in San Diego, the Saguaro in Palm Springs, Jeannie Parkman, Dana Schmalenberg, Tom Nelson, Raymond Billadeau, John Fahr, Sandhi Scott, Mark & Tobie Starr, Greg Cox, Mona Caywood, Michael Brown, Nikki Zelaya, Grandma, Aunt Marie, the Starbucks West Hollywood gang, Toni Grassi, my amazing parents and family in Pennsylvania, Karen Bilger, Queenie Longley, Louise L. Hay, Joyce Meyer, Terry Cole Whittaker, Joyce Mountain & family, Mary Ruth Huffer, Laurel Doran Lucas, Jaye & Colby Taylor, Jackie Scanlon, Lorraine Costello, Lorraine Sutton Cestone, Kenny Loggins, Stephanie Zimbalist, Jenny Sullivan, Diane Meyer Simon, Jean & Tommy Dodson, Rev. Kathy Hearn, David Kessler, Rev. Ed of the Center for Spiritual Living Palm Springs and the Docs, Catherine Ponder, Gina Roman, Jennifer Franks, Mr. Brence, Rob Lamagno, John Halcyon Styn, Damon Jacobs, John Wesley Shipp, Olivia Newton

John, Marie Osmond, Laura Wardle & Neil Labute, Lori, Jackie & Bernie Sandler, Joel Martens & RAGE Monthly magazine, Beth Ullman, Debbie Ford, Michael Maron, Andrew Page & Peter Major, Tetsu Yokoyama, Brien O'Brien, Russell Brown, Celeste & Donald Spangler, Tabatha Coffey, Jennifer Franks, Gary Tindall, Wolf Bauer. Susie Leite, Jill Messic, Tamara and the Mediterranean Village gang, Spencer Garbett, Christopher Cross, and Harolyn Keeney.

There are so many more and I'm sure I've missed some VERY important people, but that is just more inspiration to write another book so I'll have another chance to thank them!

Introduction

*"You are much too tolerant of mind wandering,
and are passively condoning your mind's miscreations."*
A Course in Miracles

The mind can be your best friend or your worst enemy. It can be the center of miracles, or of madness. It can be a place of truth, or a place of lies; it can be an environment of peaceful contemplation, or of desperate painful isolation. The choice is ours to make. **No one else is thinking in our heads.** As one classic horror movie proclaims, *"The calls are coming from inside the house!"* With all the talk in the world about bullying, the one thing that is rarely considered is that the most vicious monster, the most insidious bully, who is out to terrorize, torment us and steal our joy, is not so much out there in the schools or the workplace or the neighborhood. **The bully we cannot seem to escape from is the one living inside our own heads.**

Think of it this way, if you have an outer bully in your life, you can always find time away from that person or institution whether it is in the workplace, at school or even in your home. But the bully living in the mind you can never get away from until you begin to take charge of your inner world through conscious effort. The awful things another person may say to us, the names we may have been called, even the physical abuse, these hurt in the moment they are spoken or for as long as the bruises and wounds last. The continued torment comes from rerunning what was said or written or done over and over again in our own minds long after we have left the presence of that person or situation. And it is not simply that the thoughts are present. **The real problem is that we BELIEVE those irrational insane thoughts about how we are not good enough or that there is something wrong with us. At that point, WE ARE OUR OWN CAPTORS AND TORMENTORS. When we keep replaying the story of what was done, WE are doing far more damage to ourselves than the outer bully has done to us. We are being held captive by the terrifying depressing story we are telling ourselves. It is time to release the hostages!**

I spent many years being bullied in and out of school as I was growing up. I was beaten up, kicked, called faggot and sissy, spat on, chased, rejected, made fun of and tormented over and over again. And because I did not know how to change the mental patterns within me, I continued to be bullied in more subtle and insidious ways well into my adult years. It took me a long time to realize that the real bully was now the one living inside my own head—that I was suffering because I actually BELIEVED all those horrible things that were being said to me and because of that, a small part of me believed that I deserved the physical and verbal hits that came my way.

And because I believed those things, I was subconsciously attracted to people and situations, which were consistent with my own feelings of self-hatred and unworthiness. There is no way to escape the bully that lives in our own minds. Instead, we have to starve the bully to death by not feeding it with our attention. We have to turn our attention to the champion within instead.

"An untrained mind can accomplish nothing."
A Course in Miracles

Yes, there is a bully living in our minds, but there is also a champion. And in this book, which I consider a kind of gentle Spiritual Boot Camp we starve the bully and feed the champion. Our attention is an energetic nourishment of positive life-affirming ideas and self-concepts. Whatever we give our attention to grows and thrives. Our goal is to begin feeding the champion within a steady diet of thoughts, which will take us on an emotional journey of well-being.

At the beginning of any new program many people start off with great intentions to make big positive changes, yet they often put the bully in charge of the process. They terrorize themselves into making these changes with thoughts about how they are too fat and lazy, are going to die from disease if they don't exercise, will die alone if they don't start socializing more, need to stop being such a loser and start saving some money, need to be more successful so they will be beyond being hurt and rejected anymore, and so on. Bullies are often most active as we toss and turn in bed at night with terrifying thoughts of foreclosure, job loss, illness, failure, loss of love, and generalized panic. This is why so many people make some token tries at changing their lives and then before you know it, go back to the painful yet familiar old ways. Negative motivation is exhausting!

But when we decide to feed the champion and put it in charge of our changes, we focus on taking daily positive action as an expression of self-love rather than as an act of fixing a damaged self. We are going toward something we want rather than away from something unwanted. **The champion in us is our true spiritual nature coming forth in human expression**. Champions need daily consistent positive attention and training in order to prosper and thrive.

So I welcome your inner champion to this Spiritual Boot Camp! What kind of year do you want this to be for you? Consult your inner champion—what are the dreams, goals, aspirations and intentions for this new beginning in your life? Your inner champion can get you there in peace, joy and even FUN if you will just spend a little time each day in gentle consistent training. One thing I have found in life; we don't live the life we deserve. We live the life we THINK we deserve. When we learn how to CHOOSE positive life-affirming thoughts deliberately and consistently, our lives change for the better—sometimes very gradually, and sometimes quickly. But WE are the ones who must BELIEVE and KNOW that we deserve to be happy, joyous and free. No one else can do that for us. But we do have Divine Aid.

"God's Voice speaks to me all through the day."
A Course in Miracles

Every day I wake up and turn to Spirit within to guide me in my thoughts, feelings and perceptions of myself and of my world. At 52 I am happier than I have ever been in my life and I look forward to each day. Yet this can change at any moment if I stop doing my mental work. It's just like brushing our teeth. You would never say, "Oh I brushed my teeth so fantastically and thoroughly this morning that I'll never need to brush them again!" I have to continually feed my champion within so that he will continue to thrive and grow. I cannot get lazy or sloppy in my thinking because the world itself is a bully which is always trying to lure us back to suffering.

News, magazines, TV, movies, books, the culture, the casual conversations of friends and family—the vast majority of these tend to be voices of fear, limitation and struggling after illusions and things that don't really matter. Our mind starts to chew on these things and they cause mental decay in the same way that out mouths chew on food that will leave remnants behind that start to decay if we don't floss them out of there and brush them away.

This book is the result of my daily turning to Spirit to guide me to clean up my thinking so that I am feeding my inner Champion. In many ways it is a continuation of my previous book, "The Crabby Angels Chronicles"—and like that book, you can read this book from beginning to end, or you can simply "plop" it open to any page for guidance and wisdom for the day or the moment. It was originally written on the Internet as 101 daily lessons from my own Spirit Guides with direction for that day. Each lesson begins with a quote, usually from A Course in Miracles to help support that particular lesson. This book is not about motivation, but rather inspiration. My intention is that it help to bring you the peace and joy that you deserve and that is your Divine Inheritance. Please take what works for you and leave the rest behind.

Please help me help you. Go to my website www.jacobglass.com and click on the "Resources" link at the top of the page. Once you get to the resources page, download the free pdf file entitled, "Daily Pages Student Version" and print out enough copies for week—one per day. USE THEM each day for at least a week as a way to assist you in feeding the Champion within. Modify them any way you choose that helps you to feel good. Like anything else, they only work if you actually USE them and thousands of people have found them to be very helpful.

THE LESSONS BEGIN

1

Go From Surviving to Thriving

"The truth about you is so lofty that nothing unworthy of God is worthy of you."

-A Course in Miracles

Miracle worker, you must remember that you did not come to this physical existence to merely be a survivor. You are here to be a THRIVER! To say that you are a survivor is more than obvious. Every single being on your planet is a survivor! If your body didn't die, then you're a survivor. Even if you are incapacitated in a hospital bed hooked up to machines that run your organs, you're still a survivor. You made it this far and survived whatever mild to devastating challenges you've encountered so far—so congratulations on that. We honor your tenacity and give you due credit.

But no matter how devastating and destructive your past may have been, and no matter how "damaged" you may think you are, you were spiritually coded to thrive, flourish, prosper and grow in the Light. There is no need to justify the space you occupy through your hard work and struggles. The Master Teacher came that you may have LIFE, and have it more ABUNDANTLY.

No matter the survivor story you have, the fact is you are still here. But to declare yourself a survivor is still too puny a description of who and what you are. And it gives your subconscious mind the message that you are a "survivor" and it will help you out by constantly creating new circumstances for you to survive and conquer. Remember, your self-perception determines your behavior and is a powerful influence on the conditions that your subconscious mind will create for you.

You CAN go from being a survivor to being a THRIVER more quickly than you may realize. And it all begins with YOU, right now, this moment. It begins WITHIN YOU as you begin to think different thoughts, which will create different feelings. This will take your courage, willingness and tenacity. It will not happen without your dedication to learning these lessons. You will need to let go of much of what the world has taught you, release old mental habit patterns of thinking, speaking and behaving and replace them with new ones. You will need to LET GO of what doesn't work in order to take hold of what does. You will need to let go of being right in order to be happy.

Earth University

"There is no need to learn through pain. And gentle lessons are acquired joyously, and are remembered gladly."

–A Course in Miracles

The world you seem to live in is a classroom, a cosmic University in which souls progress through their many lessons. However, the kind of student you are is up to you. You can learn through misery and suffering, or you can learn through joy and peace. There is a curriculum set before you that you chose before you incarnated and you are free to fight against it if you choose, or you can begin to take charge of your thoughts and become the kind of student who enjoys the University experience.

Our advice is that you decide now that you WANT to be a thriver and that you CAN and WILL learn through joy, at your own pace. Choose the kind of student you want to be and then allow Us to help you through the curriculum. The Earth is but one campus within a much greater Cosmic Institute of Higher Learning and whether you know it or not, you have Advisors and Guidance Counselors at your disposal day and night to assist you in every lesson which is set before you.

This is the first lesson—CHOOSE TO LEARN THROUGH JOY—MAKE THE DECISION TO BE ONE WHO THRIVES IN ALL CIRCUMSTANCES.

We welcome you to what Brother Jacob calls The Joy Academy—class is in session.

2

Think About What You're Thinking About

"The way out of conflict between two opposing thought systems is clearly to choose one and relinquish the other."

-A Course in Miracles

Miracle worker, as you already know, the mind can be your best friend or your worst enemy. It can be the center of miracles, or of madness. It can be a place of truth, or the realm of lies. It can be an environment of peaceful contemplation, or of anxiety and worry—the reminder of oneness and love, or of desperate painful isolation. The choice is yours to make. No one else is thinking in your head. Whatever is happening there is up to you.

If you do not like what you are thinking, you can choose a different thought! You do not have to think every thought that appears in your consciousness. You do not have to be at the effect of your untrained mind. You can train your mind the same way you would train a puppy. The problem is that you often abdicate personal responsibility and do not take authority over your mental life. Would you adopt a puppy and then expect it to train itself?

The ego-dominated world has trained your mind since your birth. The ego is focused on fear, sacrifice, limitation, competition, sickness, attack and defense. These are no more than negative mental habits that need to be undone. And the best way to undo an old habit is to replace it with a new one. As We help you train your mind to think Divine Thoughts, the old ego thoughts will have less and less potency. But this will require your willingness and determination. You must begin to PAY ATTENTION to your thoughts. You cannot be lazy or sloppy about this. NOTICING your thoughts is where we begin.

Don't Believe Everything You Think

"I rule my mind, which I alone must rule."
-A Course in Miracles

Many of you spend enormous amounts of time trying to control the Universe while claiming no authority at all over your own thoughts. If you relinquish the responsibility of your mind to outer forces and conditions, you are asking for unending suffering. If you are trying to control outer circumstances in order to feel internal peace of mind, you will exhaust yourself and live in constant struggle, fear and resentment. You cannot control the outer world. You have an effect and influence, but not control.

There is another way, a better way. The better way is what these lessons are all about. We will go step by step, gently and gradually. Please do not try to rush through. Be as patient with your mind as you would need to be with a new puppy. Be kind, gentle and FIRM with yourself but never punishing.

We suggest that you begin very simply by being willing to question any stressful thoughts that arise in your awareness. You will know they are stressful by your FEELINGS first. The thought comes first and then the feeling—but you will usually notice the feeling long before you notice the thought. We are suggesting you become a Divine Detective. The feeling is the effect or result and as a detective, you are looking for the cause—not in order to find the "guilty party" but in order to clean up the mess.

For instance, you may have a stressful feeling of anxiety arise at some point. Once you notice the feeling, just take some time to quiet yourself and examine when the feeling arose and what you were thinking just prior to the feeling. Then suppose you notice a thought like, "I shouldn't have worn this today. I'm under-dressed for this surprise staff meeting and they are already looking for people to let go of and once again I've made the wrong decision. I'm going to get fired and I'll lose my apartment because I'm living from paycheck to paycheck as it is!"

Then, rather than simply believing that thought is true and trying to operate over it or trying to control the whole outer situation, We want you to QUESTION THE THOUGHT. Do not ask your ego mind because it will just want to prove itself right. Instead, go inside, close your eyes, take some deep breaths, go beyond your analyzing head and your emotionally reactive heart by placing your right hand on your belly as you ask your gut (the place of connection and intuition), soften any resistance as you surrender to the Wisdom within you and then ask:

- Can I absolutely know if this thought is true or not?
- Would I rather be right, or happy about this?
- How does this thought make me feel?
- Is this how I WANT to feel?
- How DO I WANT to feel?
- Am I willing to replace this thought with the thoughts of God?
- What is a God thought I could think instead that would bring the feeling I want?

That's all. That's enough of a start for now. You may even want to place some notes on your mirror, on your computer, at your desk, in your car, which read, "Don't believe everything you think." We are working on increasing your willingness to consider new mental options. Thank you for helping Us help you!

3

Change Your Attitude, Change Your Life

"It is most unlikely that changes in attitudes would not be the first step in the newly made teacher of God's training. There is, however, no set pattern, since training is always highly individualized."

−A Course in Miracles

So, dear student and teacher of Infinite Love, let Us remind you that while attitude is not everything, it does count for quite a lot when it comes to your happiness and success on planet Earth. You see, the ego also has a highly individualized training, which sets up attitudinal strongholds in the mind.

We could write an entire book on these ego attitudes. They are the negative beliefs that block you from living the happy, joyous, carefree life that is your divine inheritance as a child of God. They are attitudes like:

- I shouldn't have to (stubborn/prideful)
- No one can do it right except for me (superiority/ grandiosity)
- It's too hard to do/change, etc. (whining/complaining/ victim mentality)
- I'll MAKE it work and push my plan through (too aggressive)
- Why try? It never works anyhow. (too passive)
- I'm damaged goods (low self-esteem/self-loathing)
- I'm afraid I'll make a mistake (indecisive/analysis paralysis)
- I need someone to help me/partner with me/do it for me (irresponsible)
- It's too late for me/they won't let me/I tried (excuse making)
- I'm hoping and wishing (magical thinking)

And there are so many more, all sharing one thing in common—they are not Truth. They are all based on the lies of the ego's perception of life, designed to separate you from awareness of your Divine Source within. That's all you need to know about them and We will not waste valuable time and energy focusing on ideas that do not work. Instead, Our work is about cultivating the thoughts and attitudes that DO work!

The next set of lessons will be geared toward adopting what one teacher of God calls "The Ascension Attitudes"—those miracle-working attitudes that lift up rather than tear down. To make the journey from a "just getting by/surviving" mentality to a "thriving in any and all circumstances" mentality will require changes in your attitudes. And We are here to help you every step of the way. Again, determine that you are A HAPPY LEARNER and that this is a journey of joy.

"Have faith in Him who walks with you, so that your fearful concept of yourself may change."
                                        -A Course in Miracles

You already ARE changing. The energy that is being channeled to you and through you as you focus your attention on reading the words in these lessons is working on many levels. You will find yourself enjoying this process of positive change and that the better it gets, the better it gets. You are going to love this process and will find that "all real pleasure comes from doing God's will."

DECLARE AND AFFIRM:
I have a wonderful mind and I am learning how to gently guide my own thoughts in positive ways.

4

God In Me Is Able

"If you are trusting in your own strength, you have every reason to be apprehensive, anxious and fearful. What can you predict or control? What is there in you that can be counted on? What would give you the ability to be aware of all the facets of any problem, and to resolve them in such a way that only good can come of it? What is there in you that gives you the recognition of the right solution, and the guarantee that it will be accomplished?"

–A Course in Miracles

You can afford to relax when you realize that you have within you the same Power and Presence that holds galaxies in place. The great prophets and spiritual leaders of the ages were ordinary men and women with many character defects and human frailties. The majority of them were not particularly wise and most tried to avoid the calling for quite some time because of tremendous fear and low self worth. Indeed, very few were even talented.

But the thing they all eventually had in common was willingness to show up and put one foot in front of the other as directed by the Voice within. They were not relying on their own strength because in many cases they had no inner strength. Instead, they lifted their eyes up from the realm of their own limitations and looked up to the realm of limitless power and possibilities. They leaned on a Strength which was in them but not of them. Miracle worker, this is your divine destiny too. All the children of God are equal in their miracle working potential.

But you must be willing to stop relying on the false power of personality and invest your faith in the power that moves mountains. Healing the sick and raising the dead? Rearranging time and space? Being promoted and advanced far beyond your talents, background and resume indicate?

"Of yourself you can do none of these things . . .
God is your safety in every circumstance. His Voice
speaks for Him in all situations and in every aspect
of all situations, telling you exactly what to do to call
upon His strength and His protection."
–A Course in Miracles

Yes, of yourself you can do none of these things. But as you steadily practice this Ascension Attitude "God In Me Is Able," you will begin to understand what it means to live by Divine Grace. Instead of living by works of the flesh, you begin to experience the ease of "effortless accomplishment" as you FOLLOW the direction that comes from daily LISTENING to the Voice for God within you. You will find that you have

Divine Favor. You will find that rather than living by natural laws, you are living in the realm of supernatural laws that rearrange all the so-called physical laws so that healing the sick and raising the dead will now be small feats compared to the healing of minds that will come through you as you step aside and channel the Light.

This is a very important step in leaving the realm of surviving and moving up the mountain of thriving. We begin the journey with the realization that you are not on you own and that within you is all you need to make the trip. When you feel weak and tired and afraid, you will remember to call on the Strength that is available to you by thinking and saying:

God in me is able to do all things.
I am not relying on my own strength to do anything.
Within me is the Infinite Divine Power, Protection
and Wisdom to accomplish all.
I live by Grace and have the Divine Favor of God.
There is nothing this holiness cannot accomplish.

5

My Thoughts Are Powerful and Create My World

"There is no more self-contradictory concept than that of "idle thoughts." What gives rise to the perception of a whole world can hardly be called idle. Every thought you have contributes to truth or to illusion; either it extends the truth or multiplies illusions . . . There are no idle thoughts. All thinking produces form at some level."

-A Course in Miracles

Thrivers understand that THOUGHTS give rise to their whole world. This is yet another Ascension Attitude which will change the way you experience every aspect of your life. Miracle worker, until you accept this foundational principle, to some degree you will always be living in the realm of survival. Even many "successful" humans (in worldly terms), are simply high-functioning survivors. Through their hard work, struggle, strategizing and endless efforting they keep their plates spinning, spinning, spinning. They are making more use of momentum than the thriving principle We call "the law of least effort." They tend to force things to happen rather than tapping into the Creative Principle and calling on Higher Energies to orchestrate ALL aspects in harmonious, joyful and truly creative ways.

What We call the "American Nightmare," which is the American Dream perverted by the ego, is based on a terrifying and vicious concept of "the survival of the fittest." It is based on scarcity, competition and the erroneous belief that bigger is better and having MORE "stuff" is a sign of success. Some of these successful people have very little rest, no peace of mind, and are creating their world from a sense of lack and finite resources. They gather and hoard, but have precious little time or capacity to ENJOY the fruits of their labor. This is NOT thriving.

> *"These reflect a fundamental law of the mind, and therefore one that always operates. It is the law by which you create and were created . . . To the Holy Spirit it is the law of extension. To the ego it is the law of deprivation. It therefore produces abundance or scarcity, depending on how you choose to apply it. This choice is up to you, but it is not up to you to decide whether or not you will utilize the law."*
>
> -A Course in Miracles

You are either creating your world deliberately and consciously or you are creating it by default. The law of creation is as active in your experience as gravity, and like gravity, the law of creation is ruthless and exacting. Laws do not respond to personality. It doesn't matter how "good" or "evil" a person is, the law of gravity works PRECISELY the same for all and the same is true with the law of creation. When the ego uses law, then no matter how fantastic the form it creates, it is infused with the fear and suffering vibrations of the ego thought system and it will never satisfy you. When your Higher Self uses the law consciously, then no matter how simple and small the form it creates, it is infused with the vibrations of peace, joy, love, abundance and infinite good for all concerned.

"Thoughts become things" is a basic New Thought principle. Everything begins with thought. "As a woman thinketh, so is she," is an eternal Truth. The real "work" in this principle is becoming AWARE OF YOUR THOUGHTS. You cannot spend two minutes in the morning saying an affirmative prayer and then spend the rest of the day letting your thoughts negate that prayer and then expect to have a positive result in your experience. Do not say the prayer and then let allow your thoughts and words to actively work AGAINST the prayer. You MUST line up your thoughts, words and actions behind the prayer!! Otherwise you are simply writing with one hand and erasing it with the other.

And the fantastic news is that it is never to late to LEARN HOW TO THINK PROPERLY. Through practice and gentle awareness you can CHOOSE THE THOUGHTS YOU WANT TO THINK. Choose the thoughts that FEEL GOOD when you think them. Say the things that feel good when you say them. If you want to THRIVE you must take 100% responsibility for your own thoughts. No one else is thinking in your head. And while it is totally unnecessary to think only positive thoughts and actually impossible to "get rid of" all negative thoughts, you CAN learn to guide your own mind so that your dominant focus is on the thoughts of that which is good, loving, joyful and true.

6

Lots Can Happen

"Readiness is only the beginning of confidence. You may think this implies that an enormous amount of time is necessary between readiness and mastery, but let me remind you that time and space are under my control."
                                        -A Course in Miracles

The Christ Consciousness within you can handle the details of your life. The Ascension Attitude of "lots can happen" is a way of getting your ego out of the mix in designing the HOW miracles happen. "How" is not your part of the equation. If there are plans to be made you will RECEIVE them by divine download as you practice RELAXING AND LISTENING WITHIN. When things seem the most impossible from the worldly view, that is the most satisfying time to surrender to a Higher Authority. Again, fear is the result of relying on your own strength even though you have access to Unlimited Power.

Remember, you have free will and it is up to you whether you will invoke and allow this Help, or whether you will continue to try to do everything yourself. Miracles are not forced upon anyone. They come through the open windows and doors in your heart and mind. Even the smallest crack can produce results in the same way a flower can spring up through a crack in the sidewalk.

> *"Why is it strange to you that faith can move mountains? This is indeed a little feat for such a power. For faith can keep the Child of God in chains as long as she believes she is in chains. And when she is released from them it will be simply because she no longer believes in them, withdrawing faith that they can hold her, and placing it in his freedom instead. It is impossible to place equal faith in opposite directions."*
> -A Course in Miracles

The question now is, do you have faith in the problem or faith in the Power that moves mountains? Do you have faith in your own limited knowledge, skills and perceptions, or do you have faith that there is Something within you which includes and yet greatly surpasses all of these aspects of yourself? It is entirely up to you where you will place your faith today, but whether you realize it or not, you WILL place your faith somewhere. There is no such thing as a faithless person.

This is not a passive apathetic attitude in which you simply try to have "positive" thoughts. FAITH IS ACTIVE AND POWERFUL AND YOU MUST ACTIVATE IT IN THE DIRECTION YOU CHOOSE. SPEAK words of faith out loud!! Say them with the same kind of confidence and sureness as you would say, "the sun is going to rise tomorrow." Only in this case, you are being much more general when you say, "lots can happen."

What that means is, "I don't know the how, the who or the when. From where I am sitting I cannot see the perfect way and yet in this Friendly Universe of Infinite Good, I know that lots can happen. It's not my job to figure out all the details. I am interested to see how Source works all this out. I am relaxed, open, available and look forward to watching this whole thing unfold in surprising and wonderful ways. With humans this is impossible, but with God ALL things are possible. I am standing the miraculous space of "lots can happen."

7

An Attitude of Gratitude

"And gratitude to God becomes the way in which He is remembered, for love cannot be far behind a grateful heart and thankful mind. God enters easily, for these are the true conditions for your homecoming."
-A Course in Miracles

Gratitude is one of the primary Ascension Attitudes of any miracle worker. In fact, We would go so far as to say that it actually spits in the eye of the ego thought system because it is a most powerful neutralizer to the energetic pull of the ego's fearful curriculum.

This gratitude MUST be more than a rote mental checklist. Too many of you go through your mental checklist of gratitude and often the list ends with the word "but," which actually negates and neutralizes everything which came before. It's not even really so much about the words you speak or the verbal "thank you" which you profess. That is a sweet sentiment and a social convention, but it is the ACTUAL FEELING

OF GRATITUDE which invokes the dynamic cosmic power necessary to set Divine Law into action.

Remember that the Master Teacher gave thanks BEFORE he called Lazarus forth from the tomb. He didn't even ASK for anything. He simply gave thanks and then set law into motion through His declaration for Lazarus to arise from his "sleep" and walk back into the world of the living. THAT IS HOW POWERFUL GRATITUDE IS.

So We are suggesting that you STRETCH your consciousness today by practicing gratitude not only for your past and present good, but also to GIVE THANKS FOR YOUR FUTURE GOOD. Remember all that exists begins first in the invisible and then comes into the visible. It is already in existence before you see the evidence of it. This kind of gratitude takes you from the egoic realm of judging by appearances and immediately puts you back into remembrance of your Divine Source. And since the Answer to all problems is the remembrance of Oneness with the Divine Presence and Power, through giving thanks FIRST, once again you've activated the Answer instead of the problem.

Today is the perfect day to practice. Give thanks preemptively today. Use gratitude as a preemptive strike. In life, you tend to get what you prepare for and this is taking it to a whole other level. Give thanks for all the good which is going to unfold before you today in expected and unexpected ways. The whole Universe ADORES a grateful gracious receiver and rushes to give more and more and more. How much good can you handle?

8

Make Peace With Where You Are

"The one wholly true thought one can hold about the past is that it is not here."

-A Course in Miracles

Where you currently stand is where your power is. You will not find it in the past or in the future. Where you are is where you are. Wishing you were somewhere else, judging your present, regretting how you arrived there, finding fault, striving and struggling to get somewhere else, resisting the current conditions of your life are all ways to not only suffer, but to prolong the suffering needlessly.

Your power is in the present moment because your true power is the power to choose how you will perceive all things. Your ability to CHOOSE what you will think and how you will direct your mind is where you have the most power. A frantic, depressed, judging, resistant mind is not a miracle mindset.

Ego tells you that you must hate where you are in order to make a change. You think that if you accept and make peace with where you are, nothing will ever change. Yet if you really think about it, you must realize that forcing big changes rarely works. The most beneficial and positive changes happen naturally without force, resistance or manipulation. Yes, there are often obstacles, but they are met with equanimity rather than hatred. The seedling breaks through the obstacle of the earth, but slowly and naturally. The body goes through puberty with some challenges but it happens without the conscious mind going to war with the younger self.

Making peace with where you are does not mean that you LIKE where you are necessarily. Nor does it mean that you are not taking positive steps to make changes. This is more about your inner-journey than the outer one. Hating your body fat will not release you from it. Hating your debt will not pay it off. Resenting your boss will not get you a new job. Despising the disease in your body will not heal it. Criticizing your mate or children will not get them to fall in line with your plans for what a relationship "should" look like.

Making peace means the end of waging war. You seem to forget that peace is very ACTIVE. Peace is not a deadness or lack of vibrational vitality. True peace brings mental clarity, sane thinking, and it is an energy that opens the doors of the Divine Forces of Creativity where there was nothing but a brick wall before.

Making peace with where you are means fully standing in the place where you are, planting your feet there and breathing it in long enough to find your balance and to contact the Divine Center within you so that you can respond rather than react. There is a very wise Taoist saying; "A journey of 1,000 miles begins with a single step." Your Holy Guide within will orchestrate and choreograph each one of those steps forward to the degree that you are willing to slow down enough to seek Guidance and then follow the Directions as they come—even if they scare you or make no sense.

> *"What could you not accept, if you but knew that*
> *everything that happens, all events, past, present*
> *and to come, are gently planned by One Whose*
> *only purpose is your good? Perhaps you have*
> *misunderstood His plan, for He would never offer*
> *pain to you. But your defenses did not let you see*
> *His loving blessing shine in every step you ever took.*
> *While you made plans for death, He led you gently to*
> *eternal life."*
> -A Course in Miracles

Begin by making a list of what is good about where you are right now. What is there to learn from your current situation if you made friends with the present situation as it is? What can this teach you about being a more loving being to others and to yourself? Are there ways in which you are making the worst of things that you could now turn around and focus on making the best of instead? Are there people you have met or things you have experienced that you would not have if it were not for things being as they are now? Look closely for the good and you will no longer be allowing the ego to steal your joy away.

9

Take Care of Yourself

"The problem is not one of concentration; it is the belief that no one, including yourself, is worth consistent effort."

-A Course in Miracles

If you are not questioning your stressful thoughts on a very regular basis, you are in for a very rocky road in which you are whipped back and forth endlessly by your feelings. And if you are being run by your feelings, then you are probably making very little positive progress in your life in general because most of the time you won't "feel like" taking the positive steps that would lead you to the life of thriving you say you want.

Also, many of you seem to believe that if you are very busy taking care of others, it should somehow exempt you from having to take care of yourself. It's as if you think that because you feel that you are in charge of the care of others, there must surely be someone out there in charge of yours and that they are on the way though quite late. It is a lie and it will lead you to anger and depression if left unchecked. No one is coming to save you. No one can. The whole Universe can only mirror your own thoughts and beliefs back to you. Again, no one can give you what you are unwilling to give yourself. What you give to you, others will also give to you. What you withhold from you, others will withhold from you as well.

The ego thought system will do everything it can to make sure that you deplete and run yourself down so that you will be more vulnerable to the suffering and misery it teaches. It will teach you that to take care of yourself is selfish, petty, not "spiritual," and that there is simply not enough time, resources or opportunities to do it anyhow because after all, the whole family and world depends upon YOU. YOU are the SOURCE of others and how dare you abdicate that responsibility for even 20 minutes!!

This is madness. It is a total lack of faith in the real Source of all Life. This is the madness that creates downward spirals and yet it takes so little to start to turn it all around. You must let go of the ego's "all or nothing" thinking by starting where you are. This is not about a two-week vacation or even a weekend retreat because those are too infrequent. We are talking about small daily ways to thrive.

First of all, if you have a body that can move, move it! Even a 15 minute brisk (if possible) walk can begin to shift your vibration. Eating life-giving foods that are less about emotional comfort and more about clear thinking can help to turn around a downward spiral quite efficiently too. Listen to music that is uplifting rather than music that increases negative feelings. Bathe and pamper your body as you would a precious infant. Say kind things to yourself in the mirror as you would to a beloved one. Spend some time in nature. Bring fresh flowers into your home. ASK and then LET someone help you—and then decide to be satisfied and pleased with how they do it even if it isn't YOUR WAY. And also, resign as being God for anyone else. You may be the vessel through which Spirit acts in the lives of others, but Source is certainly not limited to using ONLY you in any situation. Let God be God.

As you begin to steadily devote some time each day to taking care of yourself, you will see that once again, the Universe begins to reflect you back to you. What you think about you, others will seem to be thinking about you. As you do it unto yourself, others will do it unto you as well. Simple, simple, simple.

10

Laughter IS the Best Medicine

"Into eternity, where all is one, there crept a tiny, mad idea, at which the Son of God remembered not to laugh. In his forgetting did the thought become a serious idea, and possible of both accomplishment and real effects. Together we can laugh them both away . . ."

-A Course in Miracles

War is an extremely serious thing to the mind. The more serious you are each day, the more likely that you are engaged in some kind of war. Perhaps it is war with a physical condition or illness, war with your financial state, war with the behavior of your children, war with the government, or war with your own thoughts.

War dominates your worldview in ways you cannot even imagine because you dress it up in mythology and ritual. Even your romantic ideas tend to be warlike because of their seriousness. It's what created the term "war of the sexes" though this is just one of many many ridiculous and laughable wars humans wage every day. Notice how even the concept of "reverence" is often just another way of eliminating JOY and FUN from your relationship to the Divinity in and all around you. We find it quite laughable how many "spiritual" people look tired, dour and worried so much of the time because they've forgotten to take themselves lightly. Do not take yourself seriously miracle worker—take yourself lightly and with great humor.

Now We are not talking about walking around all day laughing at every single thing you see, but most of you are so far from that that it is only the ego which would tell you that you would appear foolish if you enjoyed life as much as We are encouraging you to.

To Heal is To Make Happy

"There is a way of living in the world that is not here, although it seems to be. You do not change appearance, though you smile more frequently. Your forehead is serene; your eyes are quiet. And the ones who walk the world as you do recognize their own. Yet those who have not yet perceived the way will recognize you also, and believe that you are like them, as you were before."
–A Course in Miracles

Have you laughed yet today? Have you experienced the ridiculousness of the cosmic joke a hundred times yet today? Have you been able to laugh at the worries and machinations of the petty little ego mind and it's endless obsessions and preoccupations? Have you noticed how many places of "business" discourage joy and fun? It is why your economy is such a playground for the ego. Those businesses which are of the emerging world are places which encourage creative play and joy. They are not the places where you hear people say something as obviously insane as "you guys are having too much fun!" In fact, some of the wealthiest humans are those who are paid to "play" sports, to "play" music, to "play act."

In order to thrive, you must remember how to laugh and play as often as possible. If you are going to be serious at all, be very serious about your joy. If you are suffering in even the smallest way today, We assure you that you are taking some thought seriously and believing that you are somehow separate from your Source again. When you remember that even death itself is not real, what is there to take so seriously other than your present joy?

Your spiritual practice today is to laugh and smile as much as possible. Laughter ends the war within.

"You can indeed afford to laugh at fear thoughts,
remembering that God goes with you wherever you go."
-A Course in Miracles

11

Request the Grace Upgrade

"Ask to receive and it is given you. Conviction lies within it. Till you welcome it as yours, uncertainty remains. Yet God is fair. Sureness is not required to receive what only your acceptance can bestow."
-A Course in Miracles

Your asking implies a willingness to receive. "You have not because you ask not" is still true today. Many humans think whining is asking, that hinting is asking, that threatening is asking, that bargaining, deal-making and negotiating is asking, that pouting is asking, that hoping is asking. They are not. Clear concise asking is asking. And in the clarity of that asking is the willingness to receive.

You know that you are truly willing to receive when you find that you are consistently calmly, humbly, joyfully asking from a centered balanced place. You can take "yes" for an answer and you can take "no" for an answer because you are coming from faithful openness and not from need. To the Thrivers, "no" simply means that either you are not yet a vibrational match to what you are asking for, or that there is something better waiting for you, that you are being spared, that the timing is not quite right or that you are going to receive the CONTENT of what you want but in a different form than you thought.

> *"Each time today you tell your frantic mind salvation comes from your one Self, you lay another treasure in your growing store. And all of it is given everyone who asks for it, and will accept the gift. Think, then, how much is given unto you to give this day, that it will be given you!"*
> -A Course in Miracles

Remember that you are not asking some being or entity or power outside yourself. You are asking your Divine Self within. You are not asking out of neediness like some kind of beggar. You are going to the storehouse within and making a request for withdrawal of your Infinite Inheritance. Get in the mental habit of thinking of it this way in all of your life. Get in the habit of gently expecting Divine Favor everywhere you go—not in an entitled bratty way, but in a happy humble way. Practice being a gracious receiver.

Tell yourself each day, "I am requesting to be bumped up to first class on a Grace Upgrade today. I am requisitioning a day of unfolding ease, love, abundance, health, kindness, happy new opportunities, open doors, green lights, laughter, congenial companionship and all that Grace has to offer me today that I may share it with the world. I am willing and ready to have more than enough to share and to spare."

The First Class upgraded life looks different for every person. For one it is champagne wishes and caviar dreams. For another it is a log cabin in the mountains. For some it is a huge family, big holiday gatherings, game nights and Sunday dinners while working part-time in a dental office. For others it is single living in a studio apartment in Manhattan, night-clubbing and creating art all day long. For some it is private jets, charity work and writing juicy novels to entertain the masses. Remember that this is a highly individualized curriculum and everyone can be used by the Light precisely where they are, doing what they are doing. But please, help Us help you. Be willing to ask for what is yours. Your asking is the sign to your Higher Self that you are willing to begin to let it in.

Now, go out today expecting Grace to begin to work in your life in surprising and delightful ways because of the power of your own willingness and the Universe's unending love for you.

12

There Are Many Mansions

"*Life and death seem to be opposites because you have decided death ends life. Forgive the world, and you will understand that everything that God created cannot have an end, and nothing He did not create is real. In this one sentence is our practicing given its one direction. And in this one sentence is the Holy Spirit's whole curriculum specified exactly as it is.*"

-A Course in Miracles

Beyond this world there are many worlds, many lives, many forms of living. We know that you have sensed this at times and when you do it is often because you are in the immediate vicinity of a very active consciousness portal. Of course these portals are vibrational, as is all of the Multiverse. And in reality, you slip through one most every night as you sleep. What you call death is no different in consciousness than what you experience in sleep each night, only in the seeming form.

"You can indeed be "drugged" by sleep, if you have misused it on behalf of sickness. Sleep is no more a form of death than death is a form of unconsciousness. Complete unconsciousness is impossible. You can rest in peace only because you are awake"
–A Course in Miracles

You are always you, in every realm and in every consciousness. Death does not make you less of yourself anymore than sleeping in your bed at night makes you less of you, it only drops the body-identified self and integrates it with the rest of you from ALL your other realities and lives. If you can begin to realize that the world you see is not even the tip of the iceberg, so to speak, you can then see that death is not loss but merely a change in form. What you call physical death is much more like the shift from listening to a radio station in dull heavy mono to listening to one in crisp clear stereophonic.

But that does not mean that you MUST be limited to mono while you are here in this denser physical plane. With willingness and practice you can fine-tune your innate ability to "tune in" to higher frequencies of communication. That you already frequently tune in to the ego's frantic and vicious vibrational message is obvious by the way you often feel. We are ever available to boost your connectivity abilities. The more you practice, the better you get. The workbook lessons of the Course are one powerful means of training you to gradually open up your centers more and more fully in order to be Guided more efficiently into the peace and joy which is your natural inheritance. There is nothing "weird" or special about these capabilities to tune in to other frequencies and realities. It is only ego that SCREAMS that you must not look at the man behind the curtain.

> *"There are, of course, no "unnatural" powers, and it is obviously merely an appeal to magic to make up a power that does not exist. It is equally obvious, however, that each individual has many abilities of which he is unaware. As his awareness increases, he may well develop abilities that seem quite startling to him. Yet nothing he can do can compare even in the slightest with the glorious surprise of remembering Who he is."*
> –A Course in Miracles

When Brother Jesus said that there are many mansions in the Creators house, it was not about a geographic place "up there" called "heaven" that you go to after the body dies. The Father's house is everywhere all the time because it is the shift from physical seeing to spiritual vision. You WILL find what you are looking for. Look for Heaven and soon it will be everywhere. See the limited physical body AS the person and you will find the limitation of hell right here and now.

> *"To be in the Kingdom is merely to focus your full attention on it."*
> –A Course in Miracles

Again, it begins with willingness to see things differently, followed by practice. We will respond to your slightest invitation for Help in this. Begin by the daily cleaning up of your vibration. As you practice thinking the thoughts that the Course curriculum is teaching, as you STUDY these ideas, you become a vibrational match to HEARING the Voice for God within you. This will make you a much more effective miracle worker and allow you to efficiently and often effortlessly release fear not only in yourself, but in all those who are sent to you to be healed. But then, you've already been experiencing this haven't you? And We thank you for your efforts and ask you this question once again, "How great are you willing to LET it get?" The more willing you are to let your abilities BE USED by Us to Help others, the more YOU will benefit because in reality, "Inasmuch as you have done it to one of the least of these," you have done it to YOURSELF. Salvation IS a collaborative venture.

13

All You Need Is Love

"Each day should be devoted to miracles. The purpose of time is to enable you to learn how to use time constructively."

-A Course in Miracles

Miracles are expressions of love, and nothing is a more constructive use of your time than the giving and receiving of love. So what the Course is advocating then is that you use your time in the most loving ways possible at that moment—loving to yourself, loving to those around you. When you are not doing this, you feel "out of sorts" because you are not being your natural self.

This is also why your culture is so obsessed with all the forms of "special" love. Special love is about exclusion rather than inclusion. How could each day be devoted to special love without great suffering? It's impossible because it is a special love seeking a special person to have a special relationship with rather than the spacious relaxed open-heartedness which is your true nature. Special love involves a searching mission in which you are endlessly trying to find the mate, the right friend, the right cause or needy person to help. CALL OFF THE SEARCH dear Miracle Worker! The miracle potential is already here and now, all around you. It's the person in front of you at any given moment. Yes, even that one.

The way it works is quite simple. Each day is devoted to miracles when you offer your day to be used in the service of love itself. You need no special skills, though miracles often give birth to skills you had no idea were pregnant within you. You need not be a pure and holy person with no shadow side in order to be used by love. You need not be particularly smart or talented or noble. What it does require is the willingness to open your heart and to be used.

There is no loss in this at all—only gain. Slow down. Take in the present moment. Be aware of the miracle potential all around you. We will line everything up in the perfect choreography all day long. And you will receive all the miracles you extend today so that by the time you go to bed at night you will know that love is real, that miracles happen and that you are not alone in the Universe.

14

Stay Humble—Don't Get Spoiled

"You must have noticed an outstanding characteristic of every end that the ego has accepted as its own. When you have achieved it, it has failed to satisfy you."
                                        -A Course in Miracles

Humility is not humiliation. It is not the belief that you are a lowly worm in the dust. Humility is really a form of gratitude and appreciation. When you practice true humility, you know that you are a precious and totally beloved child of God, yet you see that the immense Multiverse is filled with precious totally beloved children of God. No one is special. No one is more or less valuable than another in the eyes of Source. All are like rays of sunlight, but without the Sun there would be no rays.

We LOVE to give to you when you are open. We love to bless, increase and work with you as you learn to apply the laws of the Universe to your life. And surely you've noticed the effects of PRACTICING spiritual principle rather than just reading about it. The more you practice, the greater your spiritual skills become and the more you are used and blessed.

But the ego thought system goes right along with you on the journey as you go. And remember that the ego thought system is all about ruining the present moment. One of the ways it does this is to keep you focused on present contrast rather than on the present blessings. Ego focuses on the disparity between where you are and where you'd like to be even if it is on the most minor details of your life. But if ego gets a hold on something it thinks is "real" and substantial—then the ego thought system really goes to town!

Satisfaction as experienced by the ego is brief at best. There are many people who are thriving but are mentally in the mode of survivor simply because they never question the ego's insatiable desire for more, better and different. Perhaps just a few years ago you were grateful that you were finally able to pay your own rent every month and were working at a job you loved. And yet now that gratitude has worn off and you've become impatient with the divine timing about some area of your life which is seemingly not moving forward.

These are usually perceptual temper tantrums that would be similar to going outside in the middle of winter and rolling around on the cold hard ground having a fit because the trees are "dead" when you want summer RIGHT NOW before it's too late!! Ego is a drama queen you know. Everything is always SEVERE in the ego's perception. Of course in truth, the trees are not dead at all but merely in that dormancy period where things are all happening under ground where the eye cannot see.

Don't get spoiled. Get grateful. Realize how far you've come in this life. Seeming setbacks come to everyone because it is part of the natural order of things. The tide goes out every night and you do not call this a failure and run screaming after it out of fear that it will not come back in again. Your eyes will deceive you and are poor witnesses to reality.

Miracle Worker, can you SENSE what is happening when "nothing is happening" according to your physical eyes?

15

A Feast of Crumbs

"Ye are the light of the world. A city that is set on a hill cannot be hid. Neither do men light a candle, and put it under a bushel, but on a candlestick; and it giveth light unto all that are in the house. Let your light so shine before men, that they may see your good works, and glorify your Father which is in heaven."

–Matthew 5:14-16

Miracle worker, you must resist the temptation to act like a beggar at the gates of the Kingdom seeking to get by on scraps. There is also no need for you to spend precious time petitioning the heavens trying to "survive" or to have just enough to get by.

You are a child of God. This makes you a prince or a princess of Peace and Power. You already HAVE the power to invoke the Light within you to fulfill all your needs. You need to develop a "more than enough" consciousness. Existing from paycheck to paycheck, from hug to hug, from one morsel of life to the next, is not necessary for you or anyone who understands Who she is.

Do not mistake this for a hoarding consciousness either. We are not telling you that you need to stockpile money or material objects. A "more than enough" consciousness is what Brother Jesus demonstrated when He fed the 5,000 with the loaves and fishes. The development of a "more than enough" consciousness is to enable you to have enough to "share and to spare." It means that if you choose you can travel through life quite lightly and perhaps have very few "things" at all and yet all your needs are met most abundantly and perhaps even lavishly without the slightest worry or anxiety on your part.

Remember, YOU activate the law. YOU set it into motion through your thoughts, words and attitudes. Supply FOLLOWS the demand. Place a demand on the law and the result will follow. But you will receive whatever you settle for in life—in relationships, in work, in health, in money, in clothes, in love, in all aspects of life. If you are willing to make a feast of the little crumbs that others can give you, so be it. But if you are ready to step out and let your life be a demonstration of God's love and Grace, to let your light shine before the world, to be that city set on a hill, then life can be very fun indeed. And you will find that in the free and abundant sharing of the banquet that is set before you, there is not depletion but rather completion.

Therefore, begin today to be BOLD in your prayer treatments and EXPECT to flourish and thrive under any and all circumstances because of Who you are and Whose you are. Regardless of whatever economic times or systems you seem to live in, you are under no laws but God's. Do not let yourself be influenced by the vibrations of lack and limitation which may resonate in your environment. Tell yourself quite clearly, "that has nothing to do with me because I am a child of God and as such I have unlimited resources and opportunities for good today." SPEAK and WRITE not as a beggar petitioning to eat the crumbs left over from the palace banquet, but rather boldly and yet humbly take your place at the table, ready to receive today's bountiful good!

16

Come As You Are

"And he said unto me, My grace is sufficient for thee: for my strength is made perfect in weakness. Most gladly therefore will I rather glory in my infirmities, that the power of Christ may rest upon me."

–2 Corinthians 12:9

Perhaps you are under the egoic illusion that you need to "have your act together" before you can really BE a miracle worker. You may be thinking that one day you will be in a better position to "give back" in some meaningful way. This is one of the main delay tactics of the ego and it will keep you forever stuck in your story rather than lifted above the battleground.

The Taoist masters rightly taught that the Universal Force of Love and Creation is like water—it rushes from the high places to the low and it flows freely into any and every open space. It makes no distinction between worthy and unworthy, good or bad—there is only open or closed. This is your daily check-in question, "Am I open, or closed right now?"

Being a miracle worker does not mean that you are a spiritual genius or that you have the answers to all the great questions of the world. It doesn't mean that you are even yet able to pay your own rent or cure your common cold. Yet still, you are the Light of the world. How so? Simple, you are the lamp, not the electricity. A lamp can be cracked, dented, old as the hills, torn and raggedy from misuse, dirty and missing it's shade, but as long as it is plugged in and has a working bulb, it can be used to illuminate the night for anyone who comes near. The same thing is true of you. And if you are breathing, that means you have a working bulb and are ready to go—right now, today.

It is a great delight to the Great Ones to use those people whom the world sees as the lowly and undesirable in order to glorify the Creator. The ones the world has no use for are the ones whom the Great Mother can often make the best use of because the arrogance of the ego has less of a hold on one who is humbled yet available and willing.

Simply plug yourself into the Divine Power Source—just the way you are, and just the way you are not. God has need of miracle workers this very day, not martyrs or perfect enlightened masters. A miracle worker is one who understands that the Divine Electricity is the healing agent, the illuminating power of the world. Again, it starts with your willingness.

And the great secret that the ego does not want you to know is that AS that POWER flows through you to the world around you, YOU are healed. It is a simple prayer:

Today I offer my hands, my feet and my voice to do Your Will. Where would You have me go? What would You have me do? What would You have me say, and to whom? I know that that way that I will know love, the way that I will FEEL love, is by Your love moving through me to the world around me. For this I am so grateful. And together we all say, Amen.

17

Walk in Gratitude

*"We thank You, Father, that we cannot lose the memory
of You and of Your Love. We recognize our safety and
give thanks for all the gifts You have bestowed on us,
for all the loving help we have received, for Your eternal
patience, and the Word which You have given us that
we are saved."*

A Course in Miracles

Give thanks BEFORE the demonstration. Give THANKS
before the harvest has come in and stay in that state of constant
gratitude as a way to neutralize doubt and fear. Gratitude
and thanksgiving says, "it's already been accomplished and I
am living in the completion." In fact, you can stay in such a
consistent state of thanksgiving that you are literally walking
in gratitude.

As you stand in impatience crying out, "when God,
when?" you are increasing the vibrations of delay in your own
consciousness and thereby holding off your demonstration.
When you stand in calm patience, you are opening the valves to

receive at last. BUT when you combine that calm patience with the JOY of gratitude, then you have moved into the vibration which matches the manifestation and you are slicing through the illusion of time itself.

"Who would attempt to fly with the tiny wings of a sparrow when the mighty power of an eagle has been given him? And who would place his faith in the shabby offerings of the ego when the gifts of God are laid before him?"
A Course in Miracles

When fear and doubt begin to overtake you and you don't think you can hold on any longer, you are once again trusting in your own strength rather than relying on the Power which holds galaxies in place. You are flapping your sparrow wings when you could be soaring as an eagle. Most likely your mind is trying to micro-manage the situation again through its limited and vain imaginings. You are living in the HOW rather than living from the WHAT.

Gratitude puts you in the what, where the problem has already been solved. You don't need to know the how—just follow your daily instructions from your internal Guidance and put one foot in front of the other. Walk in faith and gratitude. Brother Jesus was mentoring the apostles when He would give thanks BEFORE he made each demonstration. Learn from this now. He gave thanks first, and then broke the bread. He gave thanks and THEN called Lazarus from the tomb.

Keep it simple miracle worker. It can be something as efficient as this, "Thank You Spirit for handling this for me so elegantly. I am here if You need me to do anything. Thank You for this beautiful day, the bed I sleep in, the food I eat, the air I breathe, the people I love, the chance to live another day and to be of use. I place ALL things in Your hands today and cast all my cares on You. I am taking my eyes off the problem and putting them on You alone."

18

Ask, Believe, Relax, Receive

"You do not ask only for what you want. This is because you are afraid you might receive it, and you would. That is why you persist in asking the teacher who could not possibly give you what you want. Of him you can never learn what it is, and this gives you the illusion of safety."

A Course in Miracles

All focus is an asking. You seem to think that asking is a formal thing that happens every now and then, but all focused attention is an asking. Whatever you are focusing on activates the "asking" vibration. When you are worrying, you are activating the "asking" vibration and begin to become a match to the thing you are worrying about. In fact, you've already manifested it within yourself instantly. In this sense all manifestations are instant because you will FEEL like it is happening even though it hasn't happened in the physical yet.

Therefore, you do not ask ONLY for what you want, but for many many things you DO NOT WANT. Every time you terrify yourself by focusing on things that disturb you, you are asking the ego to give you the only "gift" it has to give, which is fear. This does not mean that you need to be afraid of every thought that passes through your mind or of everything that you see in the world that is unpleasant to you—it is ONLY IF YOU FOCUS on those things in a vibration of fear, worry, anxiety, etc. If you can look at sickness, poverty, pain, and such with the eye of a miracle worker who is invoking Light into those situations, then you are asking for Light and all is well. But if your idea of "compassion" is feeling sad or giving pity, then you are NOT invoking Light and are caught again in the ego web.

Again, this Course requires an uncommon honesty with yourself in order to make progress. You must deal with the part of you that is afraid of peace, of love, of having a wonderful life of joy and effortless accomplishment. This is why We ask you from time to time, how good are you WILLING to LET it get? Without earning it, or suffering for it, or sacrificing for it? In fact, how GREAT are you willing to LET it get?

Begin by focusing ONLY on what you WANT. That is your asking.

19

Be Selective—Be Picky

"And be not conformed to this world, but be ye transformed by the renewing of your mind, that you may prove what is that good, and acceptable, and perfect, will of God."

Romans 12:2

If you are going to be a thriver, you will need to care about how you feel and be willing to DO something about it. Feeling good means becoming very selective and picky about the things you allow into your mind, into your awareness, into your energy field.

Now this doesn't mean you run screaming from the room whenever anyone brings up a topic which is uncomfortable for you. But it DOES mean that YOU have to discipline yourself to not simply go along with the popular ego based meanings of things. When the world around you is full of fear and negativity, THAT is the best and most satisfying time to do your spiritual practice.

We know of a spiritual practitioner who, when she would find herself in a situation in which the voices of those around her were speaking fear and negativity, would simply mentally say to herself (or if necessary under her breath) "Not a word of Truth in it, not a word of Truth in it, not a word of Truth in it." She was neutralizing the vibrations of fear through the power of positive denial.

Positive denial is the recognition that the facts are what the facts are, but that facts are not Truth. It is not the old ego denial which "pretends" that there is no problem. It's not denying that something happened in the physical. It's not denying that there is a drinking problem, or a rage problem, or a physical illness present, or dysfunctional behavior going on. It's denying that those things have final say or power over you.

Be very selective and picky about what you think and what you believe—about what you say and what you focus on. Remember that Pollyanna was not a naive little girl who didn't understand how dark and complicated the world can be. She was a PRIESTESS who in her very first few years on the Earth had experienced tremendous personal loss and seen much suffering. But she was very very picky about wanting to FEEL GOOD and that meant taking charge of her Holy mind and CHOOSING to INVOKE the Higher Energies into every situation. And because of her devotion, the miracle of transformation rippled out throughout the small town transforming the minds of all those around her.

You have the same Power in you miracle worker. Do not underestimate the Power within you to transform your own mind and the minds of anyone around you who is seeking the better way.

20

Expect and Accept the Best

"Fear's messengers are trained through terror, and they tremble when their master calls on them to serve him. For fear is merciless even to its friends. It's messengers steal guiltily away in hungry search of guilt, for they are kept cold and starving and made very vicious by their master, who allows them to feast only upon what they return to him. No little shred of guilt escapes their hungry eyes."

A Course in Miracles

Cultivating an attitude of CALM positive expectancy will go very far in teaching you how to thrive under any and all circumstances. Whether you realize it or not, you tend to prepare for whatever you are expecting. When you allow the ego to be in charge of your daily expectations, you are always bracing yourself at some level. This leaves you tense and rigid—easily broken and shattered.

The ego is always keeping score. It gathers up evidence files to prosecute you, other people, God, the world. It is completely without humor and fanatical in its vicious record keeping. All that has happened is that the ego has once again usurped one of your natural talents and used it against you. The mind is a wonderful servant and it will prove itself right with whatever job you give it. When you allow the ego to direct it to seek out fearful evidence of a dangerous world, it will do its job very well.

The goal is to remain soft, pliable, able to bend in the wind rather than snapping off like a dried up twig. As you PRACTICE expecting your day to go well, expecting to have the Grace of God upon you, to see the good in people and to be welcomed wherever you go, to be given favor—but expecting WITHOUT ATTACHMENT, you will find that your experience begins to back up your expectation. You will begin to NOTICE that the more calm and centered you remain, the more the whole Universe offers her gifts to you.

"Each day should be devoted to miracles," means taking leadership of your own mind and directing it to seek ONLY the evidence of a friendly loving Universe. Things are supposed to go well for you. You were created to be happy. It is God's will. Join God's will for you by preparing yourself each day to see miracle after miracle by EXPECTING them. DO NOT BE PASSIVE IN THIS. Be perfectly calm and relaxed, yet alert and focused. You will create the life you expect and prepare for most regularly.

> "If you send forth only the messengers the Holy Spirit
> give you, wanting no messages but theirs,
> you will see fear no more."
> A Course in Miracles

21

We've Got This

"Simplicity is very difficult for twisted minds."
A Course in Miracles

If you could've figured it all out, you would have by now. You waste so much energy worrying worrying worrying about "problems" and thinking about things that upset you and throw you out of alignment. And the more you worry and strategize, the more you remove yourself from the realm of Answers.

Ego tells you it is irresponsible to NOT worry. That is because the ego wishes no one well, including you. On the other hand, WE want ONLY the very best for you. We are constantly opening doors for you, sending signs, synchronizing events to line up in perfect accordance with your deepest desires and greatest good. But MANY of them you walk right past, ignore, even push past because you are not alert to the world around you while you have immersed yourself in the fearful world of TRYING TO FIGURE EVERYTHING OUT AND FIX IT ALL YOURSELF.

One of the biggest wastes of time is the human tendency to always be looking for someone else to come along and HELP you. Whether that person is a mate, a business partner, a healer or whatever—you are so often looking for someone to come along and "share the burden" with you, or help you pay the bills, or connect you to the "right" people. Ummmm, hello? WE are right here beside you already, with all the resources, talent, opportunities and . . . well, with everything. And wanting another person to help you turns relationships into mere negotiations in which each is trying to USE the other without getting caught. It's just another ego strategy. People are your playmates. They are not your path to success. Let Us be your partner because We have infinite resources and there is no need to negotiate with Us.

So, next time your puppy mind wants to keep going back to ruminating on the "problem" We want you to imagine that you see Us right there in front of that problem and We're saying "Hey, don't worry. We've got this." Because We do. We've got this. Let it go. Stop taking it back from Us. You've got more faith in the problem than you do in Us. Let's reverse that. We've got it all under control.

When you are tempted to worry, just tell yourself, "They've got this. All things are held perfectly in the hands of God and if there is something for me to do, They'll let me know very clearly. They've got this."

22

Just Like Me!

"Projection makes perception . . . It is the witness to your state of mind, the outside picture of an inward condition. As a man thinketh, so does he perceive. Therefore, seek not to change the world, but choose to change your mind about the world."

A Course in Miracles

The world you see is a mirror in which you see yourself, yourself, yourself. Seek not to change the mirror, it is only a reflection, an image—it is not the thing itself. It is not the projector of the image. Your mind is. Change your mind, and you change the projected image. What you see, you be.

As you begin to understand this, it makes the correction of judgment somewhat simpler, depending upon your willingness to SEE and to be radically HONEST with yourself.

The next time someone disturbs you, whether on a personal level, or even someone you see on the television, rather than trying to be "spiritual" and suppress your ego thoughts, give the ego it's voice and let yourself be judgmental and as petty as you can. Do it out loud (as long as the person is not present in the room with you—this is to be done when you are alone) and after you get it ALL out, end the tirade with the statement "just like me."

For instance, if you are angry at your mate you might say something like, "He is so self-centered, always doing what HE wants to do, just wanting everything to be done without him having to do or say a thing, he thinks I should just go along like this forever with me reading his mind and making this whole thing run. He just wants what he wants when he wants it . . . just like me."

Then, honestly look within yourself to see where some of these very same things may be true about you—possibly not with him, but perhaps with other people or in other situations, maybe not in your present, but perhaps in your past. Maybe you don't even act on it, but you have the same mental tendency and you just keep yourself on a very tight leash in order to be "good" and you resent anyone else who isn't as rigidly controlled as you are, etc. The things that push your buttons, push them because they are a part of yourself which you have dis-owned and projected outward onto others so that rather than feeling guilty, the ego sees the guilt in OTHERS. Remember, "the ego literally lives by comparison."

This is true of your Light as well as your darkness. When you greatly admire someone and look up to him or her, that is you projecting your Light onto them and seeing outside yourself. It doesn't matter whether it is with a sports figure, a celebrity or your own children—the good you see is also a part of you projecting onto them. Therefore, you can practice doing a praise tirade that could be something like this, "She is so amazing, so gifted, so generous and kind and giving, bringing such joy to people and really she is just so truly lovely . . . just like me!" And then, HONESTLY look within and SEE where it may be true. Yes, you may not have the EXACT same talents and abilities as that person, but the projected FEELINGS you have are your own and are about YOU.

We understand, this is an ADVANCED lesson for those who REALLY want a healed mind. Play with it. Sit with it. We know that in time you will be amazed at what a FAST way it is to cut through the ego stories you often get stuck in when it comes to releasing judgment and stressful thoughts in relationships.

23

Helping Helps

"It is essential to realize that all defenses do what they would defend. The underlying basis for their effectiveness is that they offer what they defend."

A Course in Miracles

The ego is certain that pointing out errors and problems is helping. Finger pointing, fault finding, blaming, shaming, name calling, worrying, pacing, hand wringing, obsessive news watching, gossiping, criticizing, complaining, posting disturbing news on your various social network pages without also posting a loving positive action which can be taken about it . . . these are not ways of helping. In fact, they are ways of beating the drum that vibrates the problem larger and larger until you yourself become a vibrational match to what you are so upset about. You create what you defend against. We hate to break it to you, but you are not Paul Revere. You are much more like Chicken Little.

Attacking problems does not help. Attack is declaring war. The war on drugs, the war on crime, the war on disease, the war on obesity, the war on poverty—they have all INCREASED the problems and made them more insidious. Even your antibiotics have helped to create more virulent strains of the diseases you declared war on. You will not thrive when you are at war with anyone or anything. War does not help. Help helps. GIVING food to the hungry helps. GIVING clothes to the naked helps. Mentoring a child helps. Donating food to a local food bank helps. Sending any small amount of money to a charity helps. Driving someone to their appointment helps. Picking up the litter in front of you helps. Signing a petition helps. Participating in a march helps. Listening to and encouraging someone's dream helps. Calling your government representative helps. Helping helps. Calm positive action helps.

And there are two ways to help. One way is to calmly take positive action. The other is to take action with a stressful story in your head. You can just pick up the piece of trash in front of you and put it in the recycling bin, or you can do it while thinking about how irresponsible people are and how you have to do everything yourself and how the world is falling apart at the seams and all this trash is ruining the planet and on and on and on. You can be a happy helper, or a tormented angry stressed out helper. The choice is entirely yours.

Remember, all the ego wants to do is steal your joy in every moment. Don't allow this. Refuse to allow anything to steal your joy today. Your role in the salvation of the world is not about saving the planet. It's about being such a space of peace and joy that your energy galvanizes the Force around you in such a way that things get done—without stress, or anger, or attack, or fear. Only love heals.

"To the ego, it is kind and right and good to point out errors and "correct" them. This makes perfect sense to the ego, which is totally unaware of what errors are and what correction is . . . If you point out the errors of your brother's ego, you must be seeing through yours, because the Holy Spirit does not perceive his errors."
A Course in Miracles

Miracle worker, begin to seek out the evidence of where others are getting it right and beat the drum of that. End the war with reality and seek for the open doors which will allow you to be truly helpful through real help rather than through the endless attention and correction of the errors you perceive. YOU will quickly begin to see just how much JOY comes when you adopt the motto that "helping helps."

24

Cancel the Debt

"Forgiveness offers everything I want. What could you want forgiveness cannot give? Do you want peace? Forgiveness offers it. Do you want happiness, a quiet mind, a certainty of purpose, and a sense of worth and beauty that transcends the world? Do you want care and safety and the warmth of sure protection always? Do you want a quietness that cannot be disturbed, a gentleness that never can be hurt, a deep, abiding comfort, and a rest so perfect it can never be upset? All this forgiveness offers you, and more."

A Course in Miracles

Forgiveness is a canceling of debts. It wipes it from the record book as if it had never happened at all. It is the most absurdly radical thing any human can possibly do and it spits in the face of the ego thought system. This is why nothing on the Earth plane is more resisted than the concept of true forgiveness.

"Forgive us our debts as we forgive our debtors" makes it crystal clear. What you would have for yourself, you must offer to others. What could be more radical than "Forgive them Father for they know not what they do" when what they were doing was so seemingly horrendous and "unforgivable?" Remember, this is forgiveness of those who are not sorry, have learned nothing, and don't even think what they did is wrong. And yet, forgiveness is the path to your personal freedom and peace. This RADICAL forgiveness is where the rubber meets the road of spiritual practice. It is the advanced curriculum for sure and yet so simple even children can do it easily. Your pet dogs do it effortlessly and let your mistakes go even moments after they've happened.

A major topic in your world now is about debt and the economy, and We are telling you now that forgiveness is the Answer. Your politics are almost exclusively about focusing on the past, even the recent past, and the amplification of the errors of others. "You owe me/us" is the not so subliminal message of politics and economy as used by the ego mind. Forgiveness is the Answer. We are not talking about a mass forgiveness. And We are not talking about erasing the "financial" debt. We are talking about what happens first on the inner-plane—in Consciousness. And you do not need the government or the economic movers and shakers to get on board with the forgiveness plan in order for you to be free and to thrive in all ways. You are under no laws but God's. Clean up your own consciousness and it will begin to ripple outward from you. An unhealed healer is of very little use. A depressed angry worried hysterical savior saves no one. As you are healed, you create a Vortex of healing.

"Forgiveness is a selective remembering."
A Course in Miracles

A major step in the process of forgiveness is to drop the story. You cannot focus on guilt/errors and forgive. You are not that advanced yet because you still believe what your eyes tell you. You still believe in perpetrators and victims. Therefore, you will need to stop telling the story of guilt, betrayal, errors and sin. You will have to STOP FOCUSING ON WHAT THE BODY SAID AND DID, FAILED TO DO AND FAILED TO SAY.

Of course, it is not easy to drop it. Therefore, you are better of by beginning to notice HOW and WHEN you pick it up each day and then CHOOSE NOT TO. As you begin to notice the things that activate your ego about this person or situation, even if it is yourself, you can start with little baby steps. You will need to be gentle BUT FIRM with yourself. It can be as simple as this, when your mind starts to drift again to the old story, interrupt the pattern.

If you are alone, We suggest you say out loud to yourself, "NO, DON'T EVEN GO THERE! THAT IS THE OLD STORY. ALL DEBTS ARE CANCELED AND SPIRIT IS RESTORING TO ME TEN-FOLD ANY AND ALL LOSS FROM THE PAST."

25

Relax and Breathe

---❖---

"Can you imagine what it means to have no cares, no worries, no anxieties, but merely to be perfectly calm and quiet all the time? Yet that is what time is for; to learn just that and nothing more."

A Course in Miracles

Miracle worker, to be calm and quiet all the time does not mean sitting in a state of stupor not leaving the comfort of the sofa. It doesn't mean that you must move out of an urban area and live in a cabin far from the madding crowd (though there is nothing wrong with that if it increases your joy.) No, what We are talking about is an INNER refuge that you can rest in even while jumping up and down singing/screaming at a rock concert. We are talking about a quiet calmness you can count on even if there isn't a dime in the checking account and the rent is past due and all your friends won't return your phone calls.

But it does require deep willingness and discipline. There must be the willingness to see things differently than the ego does—to drop the stories of limitation, attack, defense and the sense of separation from Source. There must be a discipline to keep bringing the mind back to Center over and over and over again—to take AUTHORITY over what you are thinking. You must be firm but gentle even if you have to bring your mind back under authority 1,000 times a day. The more you do it, the easier it will get. You are forming new mental habits.

The more you learn to CHOOSE your thoughts, the more you will grow to LOVE your thoughts. You can begin with something as simple as the mantra "relax and breathe, relax and breathe, relax and breathe." The kind of quiet calmness that you are cultivating is not a switching off your mind, but rather a way of becoming MORE alert, but in a specific way. You are not going brain dead but are becoming much more FOCUSED and intentional in using your attention.

Start with the statement "relax and breathe" until you feel a bit of release. Then, follow that up with an affirmation like "God is with me now. There is a divine plan unfolding for me now and I always have what I need in the perfect timing. All that I need to know is being revealed to me and I CAN do whatever I am guided to do. I am open to the gifts, guidance and grace of God today!"

26

Falling Together

"What do your scripts reflect except your plans for what the day <u>should</u> be? And thus you judge disaster and success, advance, retreat, and gain and loss. These judgments all are made according to the roles the script assigns. The fact they have no meaning in themselves is demonstrated by the ease with which these labels change with other judgments, made on different aspects of experience . . . Only a constant purpose can endow events with stable meaning."

A Course in Miracles

Judging the events of your life is a profoundly powerful way of banishing joy and peace from your mind. It is good to remember that the Course is emphatic that of your ego mind you cannot distinguish between advance and retreat because you will always be judging on partial evidence.

To your media, the entire world is falling apart. To many individuals, THEIR personal world is falling apart. But We are here to remind you that to those who have chosen the path of spiritual practitioner and miracle worker, falling apart is really a falling together.

You know that this is true when you look back over your past and see all the people and situations which fell apart leaving you devastated at the time. And now as you look back with more wisdom and the buffer of time, you can usually see that there was a purpose and a valuable lesson in the "falling apart," but only if your intention is to learn and grow. Growth is the result of intention, not of chance. This is how the spiritual practitioner perceives things. To the normal human ego mind, every loss is amplified in order to create justification for bitterness and endless grief. To the spirit, loss is a shedding away of an old form in order to experience greater content.

Sometimes you will find that the more fervently you pray and treat, the faster it all seems to come apart at the seams. In reality, this is not loss at all but reorganization. If you are going down a path that leads nowhere, your prayers and intentions will start to rewrite the script you so carefully laid out only in order to spare you the pain of wasting more time and energy on a sub-par script. To the ego, this will look like you are being punished when in fact, you are being spared.

Learn to collaborate with Us more quickly and the pain will decrease exponentially. Detach from guarding your ideas so relentlessly and realize that We have a much broader perspective of where you are and how to guide you to your next greatest good. Once you remember again that you do not perceive your own best interests and remember that We only want the very best for you, you will learn to release your grip on people, places and things. You will thrive under any and all circumstances.

27

Penguin Power

"Each small step will clear a little of the darkness away, and understanding will finally come to lighten every corner of the mind that has been cleared of the debris that darkens it."

A Course in Miracles

You can only ever start from right where you are. And no matter where you are, or how dark things appear to be, or how overwhelming the big picture is to you now, you can immediately begin to make progress forward and back onto the highlighted route to your good.

Just take one step. We call them penguin steps. Though a penguin step is so incredibly small, the penguin manages to steadily travel across the Antarctic under some very extreme conditions and circumstances. They are not making "quantum leaps" nor are they impatient with the process. They simply keep moving one tiny little step at a time without competing or comparing. They do not get down on themselves with a ridiculous story in their heads. They don't make a big deal about falling down once in a while or backsliding down a hill. They just get back up and continue their forward movement.

Miracle worker, whatever is in front of you today, We suggest you take it one penguin step at a time. Give up comparing and competing—not only with others, but also with some fictionalized mental ideal version of yourself. Do not even compare or compete with your younger self. Begin where you are right now, as you are. It is enough. You are enough to handle any task when you do not allow yourself to become overwhelmed by the big picture. Even the biggest mess in the Universe can be cleaned up with patience and consistency.

We will Help you. We are here for you. We love you and We never lose faith in you for an instant. Now go ahead—take a penguin step forward. This is the perfect time—right now.

28

It's Your Consciousness

"You must change your mind, not your behavior, and this is a matter of willingness. You do not need guidance except at the mind level. Correction belongs only at the level where change is possible. Change does not mean anything at the symptom level, where it cannot work."

A Course in Miracles

Human egos are obsessed with the questions of doing—"Did I do the right thing? Am I doing the right thing? Will I do the right thing? What IS/WAS the right thing to do?" The ego loves these kinds of questions because they remain at the level of effect rather than cause and therefore they keep confusion going endlessly. They also keep grievances, anger and regret as extremely active vibrations. They are mental masturbation without ever reaching climax. They will keep you busy without ever being fruitful.

"I shouldn't/should have slept with him sooner. I should/shouldn't have lent her that money. I should/shouldn't have moved to this city, taken this job, said that to the children, spent that money, had the surgery . . ."—the list of DOING/ NOT DOING goes on endlessly with no conclusions in sight. Therefore you are never in the present moment, which is where the miracle is. This also keeps the ego STRATEGIZING with FUTURE plans based on past pain, guilt and loss. The ego thinks it has learned something from the past when in fact all it has done is created more elaborate defense plans and games to play to try to GET what it wants. It makes up rules for dating, finances, business, health and every aspect of life. The rules make sense within the insane ego thought system and they sell lots of books and seminars. They are basically about adopting an inauthentic persona. It's totally hopeless, depressing and anxiety producing. There IS another way.

Clean up your consciousness instead. Consciousness is King. Consciousness is Queen. It IS the MAGNETIZING CENTER through which law of attraction works. You may think that the results of your life are based on what you DO, but it is MUCH more based on your level of consciousness in that particular area of life. If your consciousness is off, you can DO everything letter perfect and still have the whole situation fall apart. If your consciousness is in alignment with Truth, you can make a LOT of mistakes and still have everything continue to work beautifully.

STOP looking for a diagram, strategy, plan for handling this or that area of your life. START working on your consciousness and daily bring it into alignment with Divine Mind. Remember, you don't live the life you deserve. You live the life you THINK you deserve. It's all consciousness.

The purpose of Our mind-training program is for you to ASK within for Guidance in EVERY situation that arises. BEFORE you ask what to DO, ask for Help in what to THINK. Ask for Help in Guiding your consciousness to the place of sanity, peace, joy and clarity. THEN from that place, all that you do will be infused with the Divine Energy of that consciousness.

29

Expand Your Thought

"You can do anything I ask. I have asked you to perform miracles, and have made it clear that miracles are natural, corrective, healing and universal. There is nothing they cannot do, but they cannot be performed in the spirit of doubt or fear."

A Course in Miracles

Nothing in the Universe is standing still. Everything is pulsating and vibrating with movement, energy and LIFE! Even the rocks on the ground are vibrating with energy. And as We have already reminded you, your mind is always active even when you are sleeping. It is always creating, creating, creating—either deliberately or by default.

You still have almost no idea of the Creative Power within you and therefore you are not having as much fun as you could be having by letting your mind play in the field of possibilities. Imagination is where it all begins. Yesterday's possibilities become tomorrow's realities. But you must begin by expanding your thoughts. You were not born to reach a certain point and then stop growing. When you stop expanding, you must begin contracting. There is no standing still vibrationally. What is not busy being born, is busy dying.

Begin each day by expecting that you will expand this very day! Quiet yourself physically and go to the Infinite Well within for the Living Waters of Divine Ideas. Open yourself to RECEIVE Divine Ideas every day. These Divine Ideas are magnetic and will attract to them all that they need for their fulfillment in the same way an embryo attracts all that it needs from the mother to build a body out of raw materials. Every single day can be a day of Divine Harvest if you are continually sowing seeds of high intentions and good works. Miracle worker, there are no limits except those you have placed on yourself.

There is no pressure or stress in this. It is completely natural to you and will feel good as long as you do not begin trying to manipulate and figure out HOW things will happen. No mother consciously knows how to force the cells of her body to create a baby. When you plant a seed in the ground you do not manipulate or force the cellular process which turns it into a flower. That is not your part. Your part is to be the conduit through which the Creator keeps expanding and creating more life! ENJOY IT! LET IT HAPPEN! It's thrilling to expand your consciousness when you let your mind wander in the field of limitless possibilities!

30

No Spiritual Warriors Needed

"Mistake you not the power of these hidden warriors to disrupt your peace. For it is at their mercy while you decide to leave it there. The secret enemies of peace, your least decision to choose attack instead of love, unrecognized and swift to challenge you to combat and to violence far more inclusive than you think, are there by your election. Do not deny their presence nor their terrible results. All that can be denied is their reality, but not their outcome."

A Course in Miracles

The ego thought system is so pervasive and insidious in the way it steals its way into your belief system that it takes true vigilance to realize when you have once again been hypnotized back into the nightmare. However, language is often an excellent indicator. Watch your words. Pay attention to the verbiage and think about where it comes from.

No miracle worker is ever a spiritual warrior. No such thing as a peaceful warrior. War is part of the ego terminology and has no place at all in God's plan for peace, joy and sanity. A spiritual warrior is someone who has been led astray by an erroneous belief in attack and defensiveness as necessary and helpful. MANY spiritual and religious systems make this devastating mistake and are actually just dressed up versions of the old ego thought system dressed in sacred robes.

The ego thought system loves this because it knows that what you defend and attack you actually strengthen and increase through the power of your attention. Remember there is never any need to fight the darkness—simply turn on the light the darkness vanishes into the nothingness from which it came.

Perhaps this is most detrimental and obvious in the ways that humans are constantly attacking their own bodies! So often humans are full of attack thoughts directed at the body with war-like thoughts of attack and defensiveness. FIGHTING the fat, ATTACKING the disease, trying to get rid of this and that. There is no peace in this and no victory. There is only rest between battles.

But We lead you in an entirely different direction. There is nothing to fight against. No battle to go into. There is no need to even fight the ego thought system. Rather, turn entirely in the direction of the thoughts of love, joy, laughter, peace and Light. No need to fight any condition of the body but rather bless it all and allow the healing system within to Guide you to the best thoughts and actions. Then, take them all with love. Medicine is magic, but it is magic that can be used by ego or used by Spirit. Ego uses it as an attack against something. Spirit uses medicine as a bridge to peace.

Again, We urge you today to drop the sword and shield and you enter the peace and power that comes from a defenseless heart and a spacious peaceful mind. And watch your words. Pay attention to see when militaristic words have crept back in and turn them around to words that soothe and uplift.

31

Unlimited Travel

"When a mind has only light, it knows only light. Its own radiance shines all around it, and extends out into the darkness of other minds, transforming them into majesty."

A Course in Miracles

Your energy arrives at your destination before your body does. In fact, your energy is a true time traveler because it arrives at the future long before your body does and can remain in your past LONG after events have ended. The issue here is how conscious and INTENTIONAL your energy is whether it is in the past, present or future.

We are always working with energy. There really is nothing else to work with since everything is energy. And We want you to begin to think more in terms of energy, energy, energy. People, animals, plants, locations, insects, traffic, the cells of your body, everything is responding and reacting and corresponding to YOUR energy.

Learn to be responsible for your own energy at all times and in all places. Rather than trying to manipulate circumstances and people, work with shifting the ENERGY. The best way to do this is to take a few breaths and deeply relax. Drop resistance and any defensiveness. Let go of what you think "should" be happening and tune in to the vibe of what IS happening so that you can to work with the chi. Remember, the dog bites the excited person. The bee stings the one who is swatting at it. CONSCIOUSLY slowing down in order to tune in actually SAVES you time, conserves your energy and keeps you far safer than any system of attack and defense ever could.

Look around your personal world, particularly at the things, situations and people you would like to change, including yourself. Then, instead of focusing on what you should DO, tune into the energy and ask how you can shift the energy. And if you really want something to DO to shift the energy, move around the furniture, clean out the drawers, paint a wall, wear something that feels fantastic, pet the dog . . . anything that allows a different flow of energy into your consciousness.

32

Divine Ideas

"The creative power of God and His creations is limitless, but they are not in reciprocal relationship. You communicate fully with God, as He does with you. This is an ongoing process in which you share, and because you share it, you are inspired to create like God."

A Course in Miracles

By now you are already quite aware of the truth that thoughts become things. Things are limited, but thoughts are are not. Ask then not for things but for Divine Ideas. A thing is like the golden egg. An idea is the goose that lays the golden egg. For instance, money is limited and can go just so far, but a prosperous idea is not. Cash can benefit the one who holds the cash, but a prospering idea can bless untold numbers of people with abundance. The same is true whether it is about art, business, romance, family, health or any other aspect of your material world.

Miracle worker, We want you to begin to think more expansively and more Creatively. This is the exact opposite of brainstorming and strategizing. (And why would you choose to create a storm in your brain anyhow?) Divine ideas do not come from activating the mind, but rather from calming the mind and relaxing into the natural spaciousness of mind. Rather than scrambling to MAKE something, you relax into a receptive space of ALLOWING. You become a landing pad for all the gifts of God that are looking for a place to land. And remember, a Divine Idea is different from a clever human egoic idea. Divine Ideas are inspired; therefore they are "of the Spirit" and create "win-win" rather than "win-lose" scenarios.

Praying, treating and affirming are all excellent necessary work for you as a practitioner, but just as necessary are regular times of quiet receptivity with no chanting, mantras, affirming or forced thinking. Divine Ideas can come at any time and any place when you are open and receptive. You may be walking on the beach, working in the garden, meditating, playing with a child, napping, receiving a massage or doing nothing at all.

Divine Ideas are endlessly looking for a conduit to flow through. They are swirling around in the Limitless Consciousness eternally seeking to be expressed through a living channel. The great artists, writers, painters, composers, dancers, scientists, physicians, astronomers, poets and philosophers were all the landing pad for Divine Ideas. But you need no fancy worldly title to be a conduit. You may be in a wheelchair with a withered body and no worldly title at all and still allow the Brilliance of the Universe to come through you today.

Say this, "Universal Creative Force/God/Great Something— Here I am. Show me Your Love. I am opening up to receive Your Divine Idea for me. I will relax myself as much as possible today to allow and let in the simplest or the most complex

Creative Ideas. You know where to find me at all times so I shall now go on enjoying my life and the day knowing that my channels are open and I am tuned in to the frequency of Divine Ideas!"

33

Today Is Your Day

"This is a day of silence and of trust. It is a special time of promise in your calendar of days. It is a time Heaven has set apart to shine upon, and cast a timeless light upon this day, when echoes of eternity are heard . . . Today you learn to feel the joy of life."

A Course in Miracles

Let this be a day of spiritual retreat as you rest in God. There is no need to struggle and TRY so hard. Today is your day. What will you make of it? It is all happening in your mind and springing from your own Consciousness so you are in charge of what you will see and how you will perceive what you see. Choose joyfully. Take a vacation from worry and struggle. You need not hide from the world on this retreat and can easily go about all your regular work duties without interruption at all.

Even in your daily work you have the opportunity to take an inner-vacation. There is so much beauty and love all around you. Take notice of it frequently today. Slow yourself down and let your spiritual practice today be one of appreciation, appreciation, appreciation.

Right now, call to mind at least 3 things that you can appreciate about YOURSELF. Really FEEL appreciation to yourself for these 3 things. Honor yourself. Give yourself the gift of self-appreciation today. Sit with this for a few moments. Breathe it in. Take your time.

Now, let that FEELING of appreciation begin to radiate and ripple out from you. What do you appreciate about the world around you? This is not a mental checklist to go through—you must FEEL the FEELING of appreciation. For some it is easier to start out with impersonal things. You may appreciate the mountains, or the beaches. You may have great appreciation of art, poetry, babies, animals, cooking, certain music or any number of things that have nothing to do with you personally. FEEL the heart-opening FEELING of appreciation and let that lead you to the FEELING of JOY.

That's it. Your special day of spiritual retreat has officially begun. It will carry you through and light your path today. We will surround you and lead you gracefully through the day if you will keep returning again and again to the gentle peace that comes from resting in the everlasting Arms.

34

Breathe and Let Go

"The body is, however, easily brought into alignment with a mind that has learned to look beyond it toward the light."

A Course in Miracles

Feel sadness and the tears come. Watch a high wire act and the palms sweat. Dream of being chased by a monster and the heart races. Tell a story that disturbs you and immediately the chemical factory of the brain begins a whole litany of processes from increased stomach acid to increased blood pressure, migraine headaches or an almost endless array of various bodily symptoms. But that is what they are, symptoms. The body is not Cause. The body is an instrument of communication, showing you the effects of your thinking, speaking, doing. And no matter what the body is demonstrating, the solution is love, kindness, and gentle correction. Guilt or blame merely increases all problems.

The way to be kind to the body is to think thoughts that bring comfort and joy rather than judgment and fear. Make friends with your body today by relaxing your mind. The body knows exactly how to heal itself, find and restore balance, renew cells and create whatever chemical processes are necessary for optimum LIFE! Your best job is to not interfere with the process. Accept it as it is. Bless it with kind thoughts and listen to Our Guidance in how to treat your individual bodily vehicle. When you accept the body as it is and begin to guide your thoughts to a loving place, which is when the body can most easily change itself in beneficial ways.

You are living in a wonderful time space realm now in which you have an enormous amount of healers who can help you to find your balance. Our Guidance through your intuition and intention will open all the right doors for you to walk through any time you need adjustment. The real adjustment is one of consciousness, but often outer means can assist you in that as well. So-called western medicine can have as much value as the shaman. Do not look down on the external form of help and healing but instead, seek to find your own inner-alignment with Principle no matter what the modality. Remember, this Course is a highly individualized curriculum. What works for one may not work for another. And what worked for you last year may not be the right path for this year.

Again, bless your body today by thinking kind and loving thoughts about it and about all of life. Make time today as frequently as possible to simply STOP the activity of mind for even 30 seconds as you breathe and let go, breathe and let go, breathe let go.

35

Rest in God

"I rest in God. We ask for rest today, and quietness unshaken by the world's appearances. We ask for peace and stillness, in the midst of all the turmoil born of clashing dreams. We ask for safety and for happiness, although we seem to look on danger and on sorrow. And we have the thought that will answer our asking with what we request."

A Course in Miracles

Little miracle worker, ask for the peace of God today and you will feel it begin to awaken within you where God placed it in the beginning. There is nothing you need or even **can** do to earn it, though you are perfectly free to interfere with it by believing stressful thoughts of chaos and pain. Your fictional enemy is ever tempting you to close your eyes to shut out the Light declaring there in fact there is no Light.

Work with Us today. *"Salvation is a collaborative venture"* so rather than fighting against the darkness, trust Us by relaxing into the rest of God where you will find the Light has already come. As you go through your daily life today, know that We are with you and have heard your request. Listen for Us and We will speak the soothing words of Divine Love. Feel Our gentle touch upon your shoulders leading you in the right direction and making straight the path before you. Give up all struggle and mental strategies as you enter a day of perfect Grace and effortless accomplishment of good.

Rather than hanging on the old rugged cross today, hang on the Vine. As you hang on the Vine, absorb the love of God and let it fill you up as it regenerates, renews and restores. Even in the midst of a quite busy day, you can rest in God. To rest in God is merely to rest your cares, your worries, and your concerns. It means allowing your mind to relax into its natural spaciousness every time it tries to constrict into fear. We have a perfect day of peace and joy to give you. Your job it to relax enough to receive it.

36

Prepare to Receive

"By giving you receive. But to receive is to accept, not to get. It is impossible not to have, but it is possible not to know you have."

A Course in Miracles

Get ready to receive your blessings Miracle Worker! The Divine Harvest time is upon you now and the only question is whether you will be ready to reap with a thimble or with a silo. You reap by your Consciousness and your attitudes. A grateful Miracle Worker can count on her blessings multiplying exponentially every time she chooses to get over herself and let go of petty grievances and complaints. Petty thoughts and upsets are part of the thimble consciousness.

Think with the Grandeur of God today and watch your silos begin to fill up with the blessings of God. Soon enough they will be overflowing with all manner of good, great and small. As you learn to pay attention to the "little" blessings each day, MORE will be poured out into your silos. For every little insult and slight that you choose to ignore and release, your Consciousness expands to let in more of the limitless bounty which are the gifts of God. As you give, you receive. It is Law. Each time you give release or blessing to a sister or brother, particularly when you believe they do not deserve it, you increase your own Harvest. For every obstacle, loss and disappointment you refuse to focus on and talk about, you will increase the speed of your Divine Compensation.

It is entirely up to you whether you will give your attention to the sweet nectar available to you, or if you will murmur and complain about the fruit flies buzzing around the glass. Do NOT allow yourself to be distracted from your blessings today Miracle Worker. Hold fast to Truth. Step out today with your arms wide open EXPECTING to be blessed in unexpected and surprising ways. Pay attention to the smiles that will come your way today, the lanes that will open up for you, the words of encouragement and gratitude, the needs which will be filled and the opportunities which will arise. PAY ATTENTION. BE PRESENT. SLOW DOWN AND BE AWARE. Do not miss a single blessing.

Then, at the end of this day, reflect back on and savor each bit of God's good Grain, which was harvested into your silo. Give thanks and praise to an abundant and ever-expanding Universe of opulent lavish good that is starting to pour itself into your silos. You are entering a time of many different blessings but if you miss the small ones, you will block larger ones from coming.

37

Acts of Faith

"Only infinite patience produces immediate results."
A Course in Miracles

Healing requires patience. Whether the healing is physical, emotional, mental, financial or a relationship, healing requires patience and acts of faith. In fact, much of the healing you require would not have been necessary to start with had you not been rushing around trying to control the Universe all by yourself. You have so much faith in the systems of the world even though they have let you down time and time again. Have you ever stopped to consider this?

Relax Miracle Worker. Let your mind calm down—let it quiet down. Breathe deeply and slowly. Drop your shoulders and with it whatever burdens and worries you were carrying there. Remember there is an Infinite Wisdom in even the tiniest particle in the universe. Life knows what to do and your job is to cooperate—to let go of interfering and then calling it "helping." Does the sun need help from you to rise in the morning? Does the tide need help from you in coming in each night? No, these are all natural cooperative processes. You too are part of this great cooperative process—you are part of the Whole. Put your faith in this Infinite Wisdom rather than in your own puny efforts.

Your part is to relax into yourself. Trust that you do not need to be fixed, but if you will let go of fear, attack and illusions, you WILL gradually change in wonderful ways. You will become more of who you really are. Your part is to simply guide your mind, mouth, moods and attitudes. Vision the best for yourself and your life. Set sail for the experiences you would like to have and then ENJOY the journey even if you never arrive at the destination. Expect life to go well and for things to work out beautifully without FORCING them to. Be less defensive and become difficult to offend.

All of this requires patience with yourself. It requires that you make a DECISION to BE HEALED—that you make up your mind to cooperate with the process and keep on keeping on. It requires that you shift your faith away from the world, to Infinite Wisdom. Healing is natural. It need not be forced. You cannot MAKE it happen. You CAN interfere by rushing the process. You CAN get impatient and depressed because it's not happening in your timing. You CAN start strategizing and declaring war on whatever you are trying to heal and thereby create all kinds of battlefields and collateral damage. Do not make this mistake—and if you already have, you can let it go and begin again right now.

We are here to Help you in many ways. If you will quiet down and listen We will bring you together with all the ideal people, places and situations that will be most beneficial to your process. There is no "one-size fits all" healing modality.

Though it all happens in mind, there are many many ways for Us to help you heal the mind. So slow down, breathe, relax and let go. We have already begun to work on you. Do not interfere. Do not worry. Do not strategize. Listen, let go and follow the Guidance as it comes. FEEL the love of God within you now. There is nothing to fear.

38

The Body is a Loaner

"I can be entrusted with your body and your ego because this enables you not to be concerned with them, and lets me teach you their unimportance. I could not understand their importance to you if I had not once been tempted to believe in them myself. Let us undertake to learn this lesson together so we can be free of them together. I need devoted teachers who share my aim of healing the mind."

A Course in Miracles

The body and its endless care is exhausting to you only to the degree that you fear and misuse it. Your bodily fears have to do with thinking it has volition and does things you would not choose—sickness, aging, pains, becoming too large, too small, too weak and so on. Your misuse of it comes from thinking that it can "get" you what you want in the world—attention, love, money, acceptance, pleasure and so on, or that it can somehow keep you safe from unwanted attention and harm. These concepts create suffering in the mind and tension in the body. They are the obstacles to fulfilling your function.

And all the while, the body is totally innocent, completely neutral. It merely responds to the story you tell about it, whether that story is conscious or unconscious. It responds to your mental and emotional states and the concepts you hold about bodies in general. In this sense, the body can become a terrifying prison for the ego-dominated body-identified mind. It is quite often the physical evidence of guilt and shame. This need not be.

When Brother Jesus says that you can entrust your body to Him that is precisely what He means. He wants you to be unconcerned with it, meaning unafraid and unattached. Unconcerned does not mean you ignore it, but rather that you respond with an unattached kindness because you no longer think of it as "yours." Having surrendered it, you know it now belongs to Him and you are merely using it to help fulfill your function here on this temporary Earth assignment. It is a very sweet thing to live this way. From that moment on, whatever changes the body goes through, you are no longer afraid. You do not even become obsessed with "healing" or "fixing"— instead you become focused on replacing every thought of fear with one of loving-kindness. There is no need for you to try to figure out what went wrong because you aren't thinking in terms of right and wrong, sick or well. You are thinking in terms of stewardship.

From that moment on every prayer about the body goes something like this:

God is with me now. There is nothing to fear.

I open my mind now to the renewing power of the Holy Spirit

and I am willing and ready for all errors to be undone.
There is nothing to get or fix or change. I rest in God.
Divine Wisdom is guiding me and if there is anything I need do,
stop doing, release, forgive or understand, it is being revealed to me
in perfect timing and in perfect ways.
I am softening now and relaxing into this Holy Instant.
I bless this body just as it is and just as it is not.
I let go of judging, manipulating and fearing it in any way.
As I breathe in the cells are infused with energy and Divine Light.
It moves into the blood, bones, tissues and organs.
It stimulates the immune system, and harmonizes the nervous system
&
circulatory system as it soothes the emotions and clears the mind.
This Qi regulates the chemical factory of the brain and
flushes out toxins and waste easily and efficiently.
It perfectly balances the metabolism to optimum efficiency.
My shoulders drop and relax as my heart opens to receive Love.
Every muscle now releases all tension and every knot is undone
as I once again surrender this body to the Universe to care for
in the same way it effortlessly holds galaxies in place.
I begin now to enjoy this body as I treat it as a dear friend.
I do not use it to try to "get" nor to block anything in this world.
I no longer fear it. I accept it as a temporary
means of communication and I am grateful for its service.
From this day on I will speak ONLY words of kindness, love
and appreciation about this body. It is on loan from the Universe
and I will never again be an ungrateful steward but instead
will use it wisely and joyfully for as long as it is given me.
If it is ever out of balance, dis-eased or in pain
I will remember it belongs to Him and treat it as

I would if it were the body of Jesus Himself.
Love is the tonic, kindness the elixir of
my life from this day forward.
Life loves me and all is well.

39

The Surrender to Grace

"An insane learner learns strange lessons."

A Course in Miracles

Do not get so set in your ways Miracle Worker. Remember that this Course teaches that learning IS change. This is not change merely for the sake of change. It is more than a simple rearranging of the furniture. It is meaningful change that is more about undoing than doing.

The ego usually "learns" in ways that constrict and contract. This is based on what it has "learned" from the past. It tries to set up control of future and present happenings by micromanaging and manipulating everything and everyone so that any hurts or upsets from the past will never happen again. In this kind of atmosphere there is no room for miracles, no room for creative living. In fact, it guarantees a present and future just like the past because through these manipulations, the past is constantly held active in the mind. You are creating in your present mental atmosphere the very thing you are defending against. This is exhausting and quite stressful. Lessons that increase stress and control issues are clearly insane.

But the ego CAN learn to expand if you will be vigilant in your willingness to SURRENDER TO GRACE on a daily moment-to-moment basis. When you resist new ideas and new ways of doing things simply because "we've always done it this way" or because you are afraid of what would happen if you loosened the reigns, then you are actively BLOCKING THE BLESSINGS that come from expansion.

Take some time this week to contemplate how you react to unexpected change. How do you react if you arrive somewhere and everything is different than the way you are used to it being? What happens when your plans are suddenly changed by someone or something out of your control? Are you rigid and unyielding about how things and people "should" be? Do you bemoan how much better things were in the past? Do you still live in fear and anxiety of the chaos of the past happening again? Are you TRULY open to the input and ideas of others that are different than yours?

The Manual for Teachers reminds you that the "development of trust" is a very important part of the Miracle Worker's curriculum. In order to surrender to Grace, you must develop your trust that God's will is perfect happiness for you—not getting your way, but perfect happiness. Ultimately, surrender to Grace means giving up control. You might as well give it up, you never had it anyhow. All you had was a very stressful illusion that blocked true learning and positive growth.

Relax. We've got you. We've got this. Help Us help you. Loosen the reigns a bit today. Breathe and surrender to Grace, breathe and surrender to Grace, breathe and surrender to Grace.

You may just find that We have a better way than you ever imagined. We are sending Help all the time, but so often when it does not look exactly the way you want it to, or is outside of your rigidly controlled comfort zone, you simply refuse the blessing and then bitterly complain that expansion and growth are not happening.

Loosen the reigns. Expect the best. Let go of protecting and guarding your ideas so closely. Make room for new ideas, new ways, and new expansion. Let others contribute and be willing to go with the flow as long as it still remains true to your deep values. We have some amazing ideas and ways to increase all that is good in your life—just make some room and get ready to grow.

40

Speaking the Word

*"And let us not be weary in well doing: for in due season
we shall reap, if we faint not."*

Galatians 6:9

Your WORD is the seed you sow miracle worker. The word
you speak aloud and the words you chew on in your mind—
these are the seeds you are sowing into the fertile ground of
Mind. Learn to sow consciously, deliberately and with great
patience.

It is a mistake to plant a seed and then dig it up an hour later
to see if it is bearing fruit yet. It is a mistake to open the oven
every 10 seconds to see if the bread is baking. Your interference
and constant nervous score keeping is actually INTERFERING
with the natural growing process.

At the same time, let Us remind you that We are not bound
by your puny little so-called "laws" and if you will JOYFULLY
sow your seeds and then trust in Us, We can often dramatically
shorten the growing season of many of the seeds you sow
through your word. In time, you may begin to notice that you

are reaping where you have not even sown. This is one of the benefits of learning to trust in Source. As your trust increases, you will begin to live more and more by Grace rather than by law. And through Grace your good is not limited to only the bounty of the spaces where you have planted.

Do not grow weary in your affirmations and declarations of good. You never seem to weary of strategizing or your talk of fear, disaster and defensiveness and yet let Us assure you that is a far more debilitating habit of mind! Too many of you make the mistake of affirming for a few minutes in the morning and then spending the entire rest of the day erasing it all with words of doubt, fear and worry. Do not write with one hand and erase with the other! AFFIRM, BELIEVE, RELAX, RECEIVE— that is to be your motto for positive creation! Repeat it all day long and watch the miracles happen!

IMAGINATION is the Creative Faculty where human mind meets Divine Mind. Imagine the very best and then SPEAK it into your life. God SAID let there be light. God SPOKE the universe into being. And you SPEAK your world into being every moment of every day. Speak your world into being in delightful ways today miracle worker! The soil is fertile for the planting!

41

The Grateful Heart

"And gratitude to God becomes the way in which He is remembered, for love cannot be far behind a grateful heart and thankful mind. God enters easily, for these are the true conditions of your homecoming."

A Course In Miracles

There is so much love available to you, but you will not know it until you begin to GIVE love without stinginess or favor. This tends to happen quite gradually and also in fits and spurts as you progress along the Miracle Curriculum. Take note of it for whatever you give your attention to will grow and grow and grow in your experience. Remember that you are healed by the love you GIVE as much or more than by the love that comes to you. If you begin to feel impoverished in any way, We have a powerful tool for restoring you to your natural state of Love without limits.

The main shortcut on the path to limitless Love is to practice gratitude and appreciation. Whenever you are feeling lost, cut off and separate from Life or from Source, disconnected even from yourself, begin to SPEAK words of gratitude and appreciation. You are literally priming the Miracle pump. Love is not something you can ever GET—it is something you EXPERIENCE as it passes through you. It is not a static state of being. It is ALIVE and ever moving, healing everything in its path as it goes ever onward.

God enters easily today as you focus your attention on thoughts of gratitude, praise and appreciation. Praise people, appreciate the trees, bless the rocks, compliment the clerks, and do not leave yourself out of the equation or you have made separation real—appreciate yourself with words of loving support too. You will find that your cup is overflowing with good as you deepen your spiritual practice of gratitude and appreciation.

42

The Abundance Principle

"Dream of your brother's kindnesses instead of dwelling in your dreams on his mistakes. Select his thoughtfulness to dream about instead of counting up the hurts he gave. Forgive him his illusions, and give thanks to him for all the helpfulness he gave. And do not brush aside his many gifts because he is not perfect in your dreams."

A Course In Miracles

The ego dominated thought system is obsessed with keeping track of the guilt and inadequacies of those around it. It is a particularly toxic habit for relationships whether they are intimate, business, social or political. It is toxic to the mind that is keeping score and for the relationship itself.

Once the mind has begun the task of faultfinding, the relationship has already begun to be destroyed. The other person can NEVER WIN in this game! IT IS LITERALLY IMPOSSIBLE for the ego has begun to delete all evidence that would show the person in a positive light. The relationship is now seen in terms of what it is COSTING and of the needs that are not being met by this person. Nothing they do will ever be enough or be good enough. It would refute the goal, which is nothing less than total condemnation of the other. It is a form of crucifixion. Now, nothing less than a Miracle can save the relationship. A miracle is a shift in perception. It is the willingness to see things differently.

This is why the most successful and healing relationships humans have are with their pets and babies. In these relationships you never think of YOUR NEEDS or of GETTING anything. You come from a place of service and extension. YOU bring your own joy to the relationship and are not thinking of it as a place where you will GET anything tangible—you are flooded with feelings of positive energy because of your appreciation of the other and since your thoughts never leave your own mind, YOU are the recipient of all the good that is given.

As "forgiveness is a selective remembering" so love is a selective seeing. You CHOOSE to focus on what IS being given rather than on what is not being given. You focus on the giver, not on the gift. What mother accepts the finger-painting of her preschooler and says, "Well, you didn't seem to put much thought into this and you know I don't like green!" Yet many of you have done the equivalent of this very thing with the spouse whom you supposedly love the most of all in the world. This is insanity.

Many times a Miracle Worker has lived in a state of lovelessness in the presence of great love—only because of an extremely narrow focus on not GETTING what she thought a gift was. All that was necessary to totally shift this paradigm was a shift to FOCUSING on the little gifts that WERE being given though to the ego these gifts were totally inadequate and insincere. Had she merely GIVEN appreciation and FOCUS on these little gifts, they would have been seen in the light of the Miracle and fed her in the same way humans are fed by the wagging tail of their precious puppy and the cooing laughter of a tiny baby.

So Miracle Worker, PAY ATTENTION to what IS being given today and bring it to the forefront no matter how small it seems to the greedy ego mind. And GIVE praise and attention to the GIVER rather than focusing on the gift. THIS is the true abundance principle in action.

43

The Happy Role

"I have a special place to fill; a role for me alone.
Salvation waits until I take this part as what I choose
to do . . . when I willingly and gladly go the way my
Father's plan appointed me to go, then will I recognize
salvation is already here, already given all my brothers
and already mine as well."

A Course In Miracles

Miracle Worker, do not confuse your role with a job, a career, or a title such as "mother" or even something as limiting as "healer." Of course We understand the value of using these words in your illusory world and that is all well and good as long as you do not begin to attach to these labels.

His Course tells you that "words are but symbols of symbols" but while you seem to be in time, they can be one of many useful means of communication. We call you "Miracle Worker" because it is free and general enough to let you know that it is possible to be that under any and all circumstances. We have plenty of miracle workers who have no particular "job" in the worldly sense.

Remember, you are not at home here. You are an alien to this world and you are on a temp assignment because you CHOSE to come here to be of Help in the Great Awakening Campaign. You tend to forget this quite frequently so We spend much of Our focus on reminding you of Who you are and why you came here. It is our great pleasure. And We can tell by your joy how awake or asleep you are at any given moment.

Willingly and gladly going in the appointed way is the path to happiness. It is not a path of sacrifice. You would probably be surprised to know that there are joyful homeless Miracle Workers, but that may be too advanced a concept for you today and could simply scare you so We are only putting that out there as a seed to begin to blow away another of your misconceptions.

For today, it is enough for you to simply remind yourself throughout the day, "I have a role in God's plan for peace, joy and sanity. It is the role I want and it is a happy one that I gladly accept."

We have an amazing day planned for you today. Would you like to exchange it for the one the ego has planned for you? We have miracle after miracle all mapped out along with limitless contingency plans for any missteps made along the way. We have a Plan A, all the way through Plan Z and beyond. YOUR part is to LET GO of any roles the ego has assigned to you so that you can take the special role that you accepted before you got here. Look for the evidence of Us today. We are coming more out in the open today to give you a little boost in conviction, but YOU must shift into a lower gear so that you don't rush past Us as we peek out from behind the veil.

44

Deliberate Proactive Play

"The Holy Spirit will ALWAYS guide you truly because YOUR joy IS His. This is His will for everyone, because He speaks for the Kingdom of God which IS joy. Following Him is therefore the easiest thing in the world, and the only thing that IS easy, because it is NOT of the world and is therefore NATURAL."

A Course In Miracles

We are the Comforter sent to soothe and uplift you. But to be comforted you must stop doing battle with the world around you by trying to wrestle it into submission. You are not meant to be a conqueror but rather a Shaman and Transformer of energies. Give up the idea of being a mover and a shaker. It is wearing down and blowing out your energy centers from mental overload.

There is much to be accomplished THROUGH you rather than BY you. You are in much too big of a hurry all the time. Sometimes you are in such a hurry that you become paralyzed and can barely move or accomplish ANYTHING. Slow down deliberately and remember to PLAY more. NOW is the time— not after you get more financial stability, or after this project is completed, or when your body gets well, or after you feel like the relationship is stable. PLAY TODAY!

We are able to accomplish SO MUCH MORE through you and give more TO YOU when you are beautifully distracted by joy and playtime than when you are actively FOCUSED on problem solving and getting shit done. We have made more progress with Miracle Workers when they have been busy in joyful activities than at any other times in their lives. Money, romance, work, health and wholeness, sanity, inner peace and Grace are all manifested most effortlessly in an atmosphere of PLAY and non-attached participation in joyful activities.

Take time today to look around you and to drink in whatever beauty you can find. Beauty is in the eye of the projector so if you WANT to see beauty, you will. Even the cobweb in the corner of the ceiling can be as beautiful as a Rembrandt if your goal is to drink in and savor the beauty of all that is in your world today. Don't go seeking joy, but instead choose to PROJECT it by invoking it from within yourself. Remember, "Only what you have not given can be lacking in any situation."

And STOP AUDITIONING for your good! You've already got the part, now just show up and PLAY it full out! Have FUN with it. BE MORE of Who you are, not less. Remember that whatever has not come your way—you were spared!

Now, how do you choose to play today?

45

Run Your Own Race

"The ego literally lives by comparison."
A Course In Miracles

"Better than, worse than, better than, worse than, better than, worse than, better than, worse than" is the game the ego likes to play all day long as you walk through the world of illusions. It is a roller coaster ride of highs and lows as the ego lifts you up in comparison to one person and then sends you crashing back down to the ground in comparison with another.

In the story of the "prodigal son" the brother who stays at home and does the "right thing" receives no special ring or a party in his honor. Of course the story of this "ancient hatred" is more ancient than that because Caine kills his brother Abel because of a jealous heart born out of comparison. What Spirit means for good, the ego means for destruction and death. There is a fine line between being inspired by the gifts and accomplishments of others and becoming obsessed and driven in negative ways by those same gifts and accomplishments.

For this reason We like the motto of "run your own race." Actually this is a "bridging" motto to use as you are being led to greater Truths. In reality, you are not racing at all but simply playing. Children running through the fields together will begin to "race" with each other as a joyful game, free of the vicious competitiveness of the ego mind which often takes root as innocence is replaced with ambition. Much of your culture pits you against others for the piece of a very limited pie. It is a culture of fear and desperation in which no one really CAN win—because it is a LIE.

There IS NO LIMITATION except in the mind. There is plenty of room at the top—it's only crowded at the bottom. The Universe is not a limited finite pie that must be won by hard work, struggle and efforting. Rather it is ACCEPTED as a gift of the Father-Mother Creative Force. When you take your eyes off the path in front of you for more than a moment to see what others are up to, you lose your own footing and slow yourself down. You ABANDON your own joy and then wonder why you feel so sad and afraid. This need not be.

You will suffer even if you compare yourself with some idealized perfect version of you. You will suffer if you compare yourself to an idealized younger version of yourself. NOW is the only time there is. THIS is the only moment in which you can be truly happy and free. Stay in your own yard. Run your own race. Keep your eyes on your own paper. Choose to focus on your own gifts, talents, abilities and magnificence today. And if you happen to notice someone who is doing a great job, use it only as an inspiration to lift you to your own possibilities in your own perfect timing and perfect ways. We are here with you. God is on the field. You are not alone.

THIS is the day you have to play in. Play full out at whatever level you are at today. Your body may be sick and in pain today, so your "full out" will be different today than if you were feeling physically strong and agile. Play from where you are right now and give yourself praise and honor JUST AS YOU ARE, AND JUST AS YOU ARE NOT. Take those penguin steps brother Jacob is always talking about and remember it's "progress, not perfection."

46

$\mathcal{D}O$ $\mathcal{L}ess,$ $\mathcal{BE}$ $\mathcal{M}ore$

"Your worth is not established by teaching or learning. Your worth is established by God . . . nothing you do or think or wish or make is necessary to establish your worth."

A Course In Miracles

There is SO much We want to give to you. But honestly, you are usually much to busy to receive it. As you rush around trying to earn everything, you push past all the gifts We have lined up outside your door. Too bad.

The hardest working people in the world tend to live in the most impoverished consciousness. Even those who have managed to acquire a lot through hard work and struggle, rarely have the time or mental ability to drink it in and appreciate it. Too bad. It could all be so different. But you have to CALL OFF THE SEARCH and SLOW DOWN to allow your valve to fully open. When you acquire by HARD WORK, you will find that your desire has not been quenched but only strengthened. The more you acquire by these methods, the less satisfied you tend to become.

Consider the lilies of the field. DO from a state of joy rather than in an effort to EARN anything. You cannot earn love, approval, money, appreciation, peace, kindness, or acceptance of any real worth. It is ALL a matter of Consciousness and RECEPTIVITY. And the way to increase receptivity is to RELAX into BEINGNESS more. Slow down, breathe, relax, let go.

47

The Invitation

"You see what you expect, and you expect what you invite. Your perception is the result of your invitation, coming to you as you sent for it. Whose manifestation would you see? Of whose presence would you be convinced? For you will believe in what you manifest, and as you look out so will you see in. Two ways of looking at the world are in your mind, and your perception will reflect the guidance you have chosen."

A Course In Miracles

At this point in your development, it would be much more helpful for you to think in terms of "inviting" rather than "attracting." Too often you still think of attracting as a kind of "sales job" in which you are pitching the Universe your self-initiated plans, trying to coerce an assumed unwilling force to meet your imagined needs. This is less stressful than feeling a victim of fate, but it is still not the place of rest and peace that you deserve and that is your natural inheritance. It is not the state of "effortless accomplishment" that the children of God are coded for by Source.

If you can begin to see the Universe as a living breathing friendly cooperative Force . . . if you can begin to realize that LIFE loves you, then you can stop all your manipulations and futile attempts to coerce your good into being. Think of it this way, the Universal Force is your very good friend who WANTS for you what you want for you—like your best physical friend does. So, if you were having a party, you would INVITE your friends to come and because you love them you would not blackmail them, or whine, or threaten, or coerce, or make bribes, or do sales pitches to them. You would simply extend the invitation and know that some will come and some will not come to this particular party—but, there will be other parties.

When you invite the Holy Spirit to guide your day, it is done. All that you see and experience will be infused with the evidence of a friendly Universe that loves you. If you unconsciously invite the ego to guide your day, then you will see the evidence of finite resources, lack of love, a need to control people and situations and validation for feeling stressed out and depressed.

You have an opportunity right this second to send out a loving friendly invitation to a loving friendly Universe—a Universe in which what you want, wants you! Do it from a calm relaxed and friendly consciousness and watch how your attitude and mood begins to shift and change into the trust and peace that passes all understanding. All is well. Life loves you. You deserve to live and thrive and prosper in all good things—and to be happy.

48

Case Dismissed!

"You are the work of God, and His work is wholly lovable and wholly loving. This is how a woman must think of herself in her heart, because this is what she is."

A Course In Miracles

The word "wholly" is so important here Miracle Worker. It's not so much that you don't feel that you are lovable and loving—it's that you also at times see yourself as somewhat wounded, flawed, broken, inadequate, damaged, hateful and unlovable. You see yourself as quite a mixed bag. And this can only be the seeing through the eyes of ego.

And in the ego's seeing that perception is correct because the ego is looking at ITSELF and not at YOU. It's great success is in convincing you that you are this finite physical body with its stories, history and limitations. You identify it as "self" and then feel imprisoned by what you have come to believe about it—what's been done to it, what it has said, done, experienced and all of its seeming "sins" and mistakes.

Your peace and freedom today comes from shifting your perception and recognizing the self that God made. It is THIS Self which is wholly loving and lovable. Take a moment right now to grow quiet and still. Take a deep breath and sink into the Wisdom within you. Let this true lovable loving Self make itself known through your feelings. This Self is ancient and forever young and vital. It has no wounds, no limitations, no sins, mistakes, nor is there anything missing that it seeks.

Make this your spiritual practice today—to see yourself and everyone you think of or see as wholly loving and lovable. The ego will try to convince you otherwise with all kinds of circumstantial evidence. Your job is to dismiss the case against yourself and everyone else. Every time even the tiniest scrap of evidence arises which temps you to judge yourself or another, affirm mentally or even say it right out loud, "CASE DISMISSED!"

49

The Garden of Plenty

"If paying is equated with getting, you will set the price low but demand a high return. You will have forgotten, however, that to price is to value, so that your return is in proportion to your judgment of worth. If paying is associated with giving it cannot be perceived as loss, and the reciprocal relationship of giving and receiving will be recognized. The price will then be set high, because of the value of the return . . . Never forget, then, that you set the value on what you receive, and price it by what you give. To believe that it is possible to get much for little is to believe that you can bargain with God."

A Course In Miracles

When you go in search of bargains, you diminish your own prosperity. Trying to receive the most while giving the least is NOT an abundance principle—it is the root of scarcity. In fact, if you are waiting to receive something today, most likely you will be waiting 10 years from now too. Remember, a "get" mentality is not a receptive mentality. A GIVE mentality is the priming of the pump and is the root of an open receptive state of being.

If you are in lack and live in such a way that you are waiting for others to give to you, you do not understand the most basic laws of the Universe and are living by the flesh and not by the spirit. We see this in spiritual groups all the time. Those who do not give today are still not giving 10 years later—AND they have even less to give. They have not sown the seeds necessary to bring in a harvest and their garden gradually grows smaller and more barren as the years go by.

You reap what you sow. If you sow service, you will reap a harvest of those willing to help you. If you sow kindness, you will reap a harvest of those who are kind to you. If you sow fear, you will reap a harvest of terrifying thoughts. If you sow money, you will reap a harvest of money. A tree is known by the fruit it bears. You do not sow apples seeds and reap tomatoes. Principle is very simple. It is ego that is complex and always trying to strategize a deal with the Universe—a bargaining that does not work.

When you begin to GIVE the very thing you want, your garden will begin to flourish and grow in glorious and unexpected ways. IF you are waiting for something today, find a way to give that very thing first as your act of faith, as the seed you sow. There is no harvest without planting.

50

Praising the Good

"Beware of the temptation to perceive yourself unfairly treated."

A Course In Miracles

Praising the good is praising God. Whatever you are giving attention to and focusing on is going to increase in your awareness. It will virtually wallpaper your mind the more you focus on it. NEVER EVER SPEAK OF LACK OR DECLINE IN ANY WAY WHATSOEVER unless you WANT that lack and decline!! This cannot be too emphatically stated!

If you want to talk about the decline of your debt, then that is fine because it will hasten it disappearing. If you want to speak of the lack and decline of some old chronic physical ailment as it retreats from your experience that is fine as well. But that is still not the path to positive growth and expansion of the miraculous bountiful good that is waiting to be poured out upon you. There is a better way . . .

You must be AGGRESSIVELY grateful and positive when the ego begins to introduce fear thoughts into a particular situation or area of your life. YOU CANNOT BE LAZY OR SLOPPY ABOUT THIS! It is only a temporary measure while you pass through the temptation of the valley. The fastest way to be aggressively positive is through praise, gratitude and appreciation. Making lists of the positive aspects of even your most fearful situations can be the very thing that allows you to turn the corner from fear-based ego thinking to the peace and power of the true thoughts of God.

You need not always be so aggressive. In fact, walking in a gentle peace and love is much more your natural state of being. But when the ego has begun to build a fortress in some area of your life and is beginning to bombard you with attack thoughts, it takes an aggressive counter-force in the direction of Truth. An assertive and aggressive gratitude can be the very thing that turns the tide.

Nothing is more dangerous to the mind of the miracle worker than fearful self-pity and victim consciousness! Therefore, when this occurs it must be vigorously addressed as soon as possible with the neutralizing remedy of praise, gratitude and appreciation along with making a DELIBERATE CHOICE in how you want to feel and what thoughts you are choosing to strengthen in your own mind. Remember, the motto is "listen, learn and DO!"

51

The Real Currency

"Seek not outside yourself. For it will fail, and you will weep each time an idol falls. Heaven cannot be found where it is not, and there can be no peace excepting there. Each idol that you worship when God calls will never answer in His place. There is no other answer you can substitute, and find the happiness His answer brings."

A Course In Miracles

Too many miracle workers are leaking and spewing energy all over the place as they go through their days and nights. In fact, you need not even leave your sofa to be leaking enormous amounts of energy. RETRACT YOUR ENERGY miracle worker! Call it back to you now and become self centered, meaning centered in your Self. STOP being outwardly centered. It leaves no one at home within YOU and this is why you feel so easily abandoned. You abandon yourself many many times a day. Come home.

God is Pure Positive Energy. And everything is made OF Energy. This is what you are and what all Life is. The things of the world are nothing more or less than the avenues through which that Energy is expressing Itself. You try too hard to master the avenues when your time and focus should be turned toward mastering your Energy!

True wealth, prosperity and abundance are not about money—it is about ENERGY. This is why so many of the monetary systems of the world are in such an upheaval now. It is the falling of yet another ego idol. ALL idols fall, over and over and over again. This will never end. It must be. No idol can stand the test of time.

You will find in Matthew 27:17 that Brother Jesus paid his taxes by taking the money from the mouth of a fish which he instructed Peter to catch. Manna fell from the sky to feed the Israelites every day while they were in the desert for decades. The day will come when you see these things as quite ordinary—but only when you stop wasting your energy in trying to "get" and manifest money, mates, health, jobs, babies and the AVENUES of energy rather than mastering the Energy Itself within you.

As you begin to master Energy, you will notice that your needs are effortlessly and joyfully taken care of whether money is involved or not. We do not mean that you will manage to scrape by making do with what others are willing to give to you. We do not mean that you will start to "barter" to get your needs met, for this is just another strategic form of egoic idolatry dressed up in hippie clothes.

When you think that money is currency, you have a fearful consciousness around it whether you have a lot of it or none at all. You endlessly count it, hoard it, waste it, think about it, yearn for it, feel guilty about it, judge and hate it . . . THIS IS IDOLATRY! It makes you miserable and depressed.

CALL BACK YOUR ENERGY—RETRACT IT today and stay centered within your Self. There is absolutely nothing happening outside of you. Every time you notice that your mind has wandered outside of you and you have put your Energy into someone or something "out there"—STOP!! Take a deep breath and bring it back to yourself again. Then tell yourself firmly and clearly, "I always have what I need for I live in a Universe of abundant lavish good. I will always have more than enough good to share and to spare."

A wonderful home, transportation, abundant health and vitality, love and acknowledgment, resources and opportunities, travel, romance, family, and yes even money—any and all of these will be the various temporary forms that the Energy will take in your life as you walk the path. But the MOMENT you begin to think the thing is Source, it will start to fall apart. If you think your husband is the source of your lovely home and family, you are already in a pretty prison in hell—and still you will weep when this idol falls, which it will—unless you get the lesson now and make the correction to put God at the center of your life rather than the various forms of God Energy. This is not because God is "jealous"—it is not God's doing. It is simply the natural result of putting your power in anything outside of you. The Kingdom is within you—that's all. Call back your Energy to yourself a thousand and one times today miracle worker. It is the only currency there is.

52

What Is Not Given Is Lost

"Who understands what giving means must laugh at the idea of sacrifice."

A Course In Miracles

There are two main energy patterns in the Universe—circulation and congestion. Circulation is movement, givingness, health, vitality, prosperity, renewal—it is the energy of thriving. Congestion is stagnant, blocked, fetid, hoarding—it is the energy of lack leading to decay.

Bodies want movement, relationships require ongoing love deposits, careers need activity, money needs to be used, the good dishes need to be eaten on—Life offers itself to those who are using It up on a regular basis. Storage facilities are for those who are not interested in thriving anymore. Sedentary bodies are for those who are interested in seeing what decay feels like—if all you can move are your arms, they need to move!

"Use it or lose it" is a basic tenet of this energy principle of circulation and congestion. The Tao flows to wherever there is an open space to enter. It is no respecter of persons or personalities. The more you use, the more is poured out upon you. "Them that's got shall get, them that's not shall lose" is more than a song lyric, it is an eternal truth. What you hold onto will rot and turn to dust in your hands. What you release, keeps returning and returning and returning. But YOU must have eyes to perceive it, and be open to let it in!

53

Just Sayin

"No evidence will convince you of the truth of what you do not want."

A Course In Miracles

We watch so many of you wrestling with Principle, trying to fool the Universe or making endless compromises with Principle, adapting them to your ego's liking so that no real change is required of you and then wondering why you have so little spiritual Power flowing through you. It would be laughable if it did not cause you so much frustration and suffering.

You only cheat yourself when you pick and choose the Principles that you prefer. Living with one foot in God's world and one foot in the world of the flesh is a high anxiety, high stress way to go through life. More than that, it dilutes both worlds so that you never receive the full "gifts" of either realm because of the watering down process.

You have been given the freedom of the lesson, "I am under no laws but God's" but the question is do you really BELIEVE it as a way of life or is it yet another sweet spiritual motto you say only in the gravest of emergencies when all other worldly ways have failed? The vision of one world costs you the vision of the other. You cannot serve two masters. A house divided cannot stand. Ego or Divine Mind is the choice. Going back and forth over and over and over all day long—or trying to broker deals between them where you still do some things by the "rules" of the illusory physical realm and do other things by the Laws of God is like riding the worst roller coaster in the Universe. It's why many of you have so many problems sleeping at night.

Make a decision—one world or the other. Then go for it all the way.

54

The Lessons of Love

"Put yourself not in charge of this, for you cannot distinguish between advance and retreat. Some of your greatest advances you have judged as failures, and some of your deepest retreats you have evaluated as success."

A Course In Miracles

Body identification and the egoic obsession with form is what makes learning so difficult. Simply put, you judge according to appearances and not by content. In relationships this is how you tend to judge the so-called success or failure of them. You look to the body, to the length of time of a particular form of the relationship, to how it "ended" and who was to "blame" for the failures. These are the criteria by which the ego evaluates and judges.

Let Us make this clear to you now; form and time have NOTHING whatsoever to do with the success or failure of a relationship. The only failure in relationship is failure to learn. EVERY relationship is a lesson of love, including your "special hate" relationships. What this means is that any relationship can be a success even decades after the form has ended. All that is necessary is that you choose NOW to learn the lesson of love that was presented then. It is never too late to learn. In this sense, nothing is ever truly over because it lives on in mind and every moment is an opportunity to allow the Holy Spirit to help you reinterpret everything that was fear into a present love.

This is very important—you must ask Holy Spirit to help you learn this. Any "lesson" that you learned from a relationship about being more guarded, less open, more defensive, more prideful and so on—these are NOT lessons and that was failure to learn. This is why you must not be your own teacher of love but must ASK Spirit to guide your thoughts, feelings and perceptions so that you may see true lesson of love. Perhaps what you learned was that you were being unkind and unloving to yourself by remaining in a situation that did not serve you. The ego twists this to say the lesson is that the other person is horrible and dangerous and you must guard yourself against the abusers of the world. But remember, you create what you defend against. When you go out into the world with your guard up, you have trapped yourself in the prison with the real abuser—your defensive ego mind.

Lessons of love are never about fear and defensiveness. And it is only by looking beyond the body and form that you can truly become fearless enough to be teachable so that you walk through the world as a Master of Love.

55

Happy Games

"If I defend myself I am attacked. But in my
defenselessness I will be strong, and I will learn what
my defenses hide."

A Course In Miracles

There is no risk in love—except to the ego. The Course
emphasizes that "the ego is certain that love is dangerous" and
indeed love is quite dangerous to the ego. In the presence of
Love, the ego dissolves and because of this the ego has built
elaborate mental fortresses to keep love at a safe distance even
while keeping the body of the loved ones quite near.

To the ego, embarrassment is a very intense form of
crucifixion. Because of this the ego is very defensive about:
looking foolish, being made a fool of, being taken advantage
of, being used, revealing too much, being naked emotionally,
loving more than one is loved, giving too much, and all manner
of thoughts that come down to a basic problem of pride and
defensiveness.

Therefore, let us again make the example of your relationships with babies and pets and why they inspire such joyful love in you. No one is afraid of looking foolish in front of the dog. No one is afraid that the baby is winning the power struggle because you've been too vulnerable and given her the upper hand. And this is NOT because you know your pet or baby cannot walk out on you or that the baby is seeing other mommies behind your back. After all, you will act silly with an infant you see in the elevator or with a stranger's puppy at the coffee shop and yet you've made no deal with them that they will never abandon you.

It's a simple matter of projection. You don't project fear-based painful fantasies, myths, fairy tales, business models, relationship strategies, and your own unforgiven past onto babies and pets. Therefore, you are IN the Holy Instant with them and you drop all YOUR defenses and are completely available to the love that is present because you are focused on GIVING it. You are not in some story in your head about how to GET your needs met or how to protect yourself from harm. You become gentle and harmless, and because the Universe is a mirror, when you are profoundly harmless, you cannot BE harmed. Nothing is EVER happening outside of you.

Love is not stupid or foolish. Love is visionary and wise. But often what you call love is bargaining and NEEDINESS and fear. Defenseless love does not mean that you go into business partnership just because someone asks you to, that you lend a loved one thousands of dollars, that you allow him to move back in with you, that you drop the legal charges against the child molester . . . it means that you honor yourself as much as the other because you are not separate. You SEEK Guidance from the Source within you about behavior while never closing your heart.

Transformative Love is not for people who want to maintain their act of looking cool and in control. It is not for people who want to stay in the power struggle. It is not for those who want the illusion of safety for their ego. Joyful love is about playing a game in which everyone wins and no one loses.

56

The Correction Ratio

"To the ego it is kind and good to point out errors and "correct" them. This makes perfect sense to the ego, which is unaware of what errors are and what correction is . . . Any attempt you make to correct a brother means that you believe correction by you is possible, and this can only be the arrogance of the ego."

A Course In Miracles

Relationships as seen through the eyes of the ego can deplete your energy and exhaust you beyond measure. They can seem to literally suck the energy out of you as you focus on DOING all the "right" things in an attempt to control yourself, the other, or to "fix" the relationship. In your mechanistic worldview, many of you treat everything as a kind of machine that you are forever tinkering with the parts of in order to manipulate it into working as YOU think it "should."

To the Holy Spirit within you, relationships are not machines but rather the garden of miracles. They are the gateway to an energy that is beyond the body and beyond this world's limits entirely. And the only way to know this is through practicing acceptance rather than resistance. Acceptance is a matter of surrender and trust. As you surrender yourself, the other, and the relationship itself to the Holy Spirit within you, you can finally know true rest and rejuvenation.

This is not a hopeless giving in to accepting that you are just going to have to suffer your way through to the end. That is surrendering to your ego rather than surrendering to Spirit. When you surrender to Spirit you are trusting that the Universe loves you and has a perfect plan to guide you and your relationship IF you will simply let go and LISTEN for instruction.

When you turn to Us as your messengers of God, 99% of the time We are going to tell you "Don't worry, We've got this!" And then your job is to simply keep knowing and affirming that God is on the field. Your file has not been lost. If there is something for you to do, We'll align things in such a way that you will go in that direction without stress, anxiety or tension.

In the meantime, stay in your own yard and keep it nice and clean instead of spending so much time focusing on what you think others need to be doing or not doing in theirs. This keeps you from spewing your energy and leaking it all over the place as you try to control that which is beyond your control.

BUT, since you are all so DOING oriented, let us give you a simple little formula to work with that will help you immeasurably. For every helpful suggestion that you give to "correct" someone, you must FIRST give 99 compliments and words of lavish praise. That's the ratio. You will find that all this lavish praise and words of encouragement, love and support build up a kind of emotional bank account which allows you to make the withdrawal of your "helpful" correction every now and then. When you are constantly "helping" someone with your advice, they quickly begin to tune you out. But if you are someone who has always been very encouraging and supportive—on a daily basis—in WORDS and actions—then when you DO have something that you legitimately need to say to that person, their ego is far less likely to become defensive and they are much more likely to LISTEN to you with an open heart.

Work with that for 6 months and keep a record of the miracles that come from this shift as well as of what you learn from the practice. This is graduate level lab work and yet again it is simple, simple, simple.

57

A Smile Millionaire

"The correction of fear is your responsibility. When you ask for release from fear, you are implying that it is not. You should ask, instead, for help in the conditions that have brought the fear about. These conditions always entail a willingness to be separate. At that level you can help it. You are much too tolerant of mind wandering and are passively condoning your mind's miscreations."

A Course In Miracles

Loneliness is a choice, like everything else. It is not a conscious choice, but it is a choice just the same. It is the choice to give in to fear and separation. It is passively allowing ego to steal away your joy.

We see so many humans walking the cities, complaining about loneliness while surrounded by millions of people! But the Truth is that those who complain of loneliness are not a vibrational match to congenial companionship. Many of them are vain, unfriendly and give off an energy that says DON'T TALK TO ME!! They walk the world in a cloud of their own dark thoughts and obsessions. They are not available as they desperately tell themselves that they WANT someone to love. They are desperately seeking for someone WORTHY of their attention as they pass people by all day long whom they see as not good enough or too good for them, not safe, too different . . . separate, separate, separate. If they do happen upon someone they see as good enough or desirable, they are too afraid to do anything about it, or so desperately hungry for love that they often terrify the person away.

When you walk the world passing by people because you think they "don't count" somehow, you are denying yourself your daily bread. As you look around for only those who look like you, think like you, vote like you, act like you, have a body like yours, are at your same socio-economic level and so on . . . well, you are rejecting most of your world. And those who reject, will always FEEL rejected. Remember, your thoughts never leave your own mind. All that you withhold will be withheld from you. All that you give is ultimately given to yourself.

Spiritual and religious groups are no better. The same divisions and separations happen in every Earthly environment. Separation is always always a choice. But you CAN change your mind. You CAN make a better decision, a different choice. Shyness is nothing more than another ego excuse for investing in separation—it is part of the personal mythology the ego clings to in misery. HOW you got so afraid or separate is 100% irrelevant. It is just the OLD story you tell to justify and argue for your limitations. Throw it out now and become a smile millionaire.

That means drop your armor and your attitude. Cultivate a friendly non-attached smile. Make friends with Life. Get out of the cave of your mind as you walk the world and start ENGAGING with people if you want to see the end of loneliness. As you well know, you can be just as lonely in a marriage as you can sitting in a room all by yourself. Loneliness is simply the willingness to see yourself as separate. You are NOT separate from Life or from the whole anymore than a wave can be separate from the ocean. STOP saying you are lonely and START smiling and saying hello to a world of people who are right outside your front door. People may think you are crazy and have lost your mind—sanity looks crazy in an insane world. That's fine—it means you won't be a vibrational match to others who are practicing unfriendliness and separation!

Become a smile millionaire today and go out to spread the wealth! Give away as many genuine smiles as possible today and you will be receiving your own daily bread. Soon enough you will find it impossible to honestly say that you are ever lonely.

58

The Proof is in the Fruitage

"To teach is to demonstrate. There are only two thought systems, and you demonstrate that you believe one or the other is true all the time. From your demonstration others learn, and so do you . . . you cannot give to someone else, but only to yourself, and this you learn through teaching. Teaching is but a call to witnesses to attest to what you believe."

A Course In Miracles

Of course these two thought systems are love or fear, Truth or illusions, abundance or scarcity, Life or death. You teach not by what you say, but by how you actually live. Philosophy is all well and good, but unless you can live it . . . well, talk is cheap. A tree is known by the fruit it bears, not by words. An apple tree may have a sign under it that reads, "Pear Tree"—but that tree will go right on bearing apples, apples, apples.

Choosing to teach love today means you have decided to demonstrate love. We are not talking about sentimentality and fluff here. This means love IN ACTION, for yourself and for all those who cross your path or your mind today. That means you begin to let go of the mythology of love and whatever foolish beliefs the culture teaches about love.

For instance, "putting others first" is taught as a kind of loving spiritual value. It is not. It is yet another ego concept. If you put others first, it means you must be separate from others and THIS IS the very foundation of the entire ego thought system. Real love neither puts self nor others first. Love simply answers the call for love wherever it is made whether by the seeming self, or the seeming other. NO SEPARATION. Love gives without sacrifice and receives without guilt. It is all equal, equal, equal.

Ultimately you come to realize that there is nothing and no one outside of you—therefore, all that you give is given to yourself. And this you learn by teaching it to yourself through your own demonstration. We will provide the endless opportunities to joyfully learn this if that is what you choose. Remember, you can learn through joy or through pain and which path you choose each moment is entirely up to you. We are here to Help you as much as you will allow.

Let Us Help you teach love today. Life can be so fun. Love can be so delightful when you drop the ego illusions about it. Demonstrate today that Love is about a light heart and a joyful attitude. Teach it to yourself and your influence will ripple out across the Cosmic Ocean to all those who thirst for Living Water. THIS is a great day in your learning BECAUSE of what you have chosen to teach.

59

The Doorway Marked "Death"

"Yet there is a kind of seeming death that has a different source. It does not come because of hurtful thoughts and raging anger at the universe. It merely signifies the end has come for usefulness of body functioning. And so it is discarded as a choice, as one lays by a garment now outworn."

A Course In Miracles

Of course this laying aside of the body as a choice is rarely a conscious choice. The choice is made on a much deeper subconscious level for the vast majority of humans. But regardless of how the choice is made, death is merely a word the ego uses to terrify you because of its obsession with body identification. It seems to be the end of YOU, but it is no more the end of you or a loss of self than it is when you take off that beloved sweater and throw it on the bed.

In reality, death is nothing more than going from one room into another—one classroom to another—one frequency to another. It is not a punishment nor a failure. It is simply the way one leaves this school for a while between semesters.

When one of your loved ones seems to "die" it feels as if they have abandoned you. In fact, YOU abandon them because you stop communicating. They are not dead, only "dead to you" because you think that communication is of the body. To Us this is as silly as talking to that sweater. The body was never a truly living thing any more than a hand puppet or marionette is a living thing. Fascinating, fun, a creative vessel, yes! But never a truly living thing.

What animated the body is as alive and vibrant as ever and even more so because there are none of the limitations of the instrument to seem to inhibit full expression. Your loved ones are now in a state of joyous limitless energy and in order to communicate with them fully, you must begin to match that same frequency. When you are in sadness and grief and loss, it is very difficult to "hear" your loved ones because that is not the station they are broadcasting on.

Instead, relax very deeply, become one with your happiest memories together—THAT is the meeting place. In this place, beyond the body and it's serial adventures, is the place of happy clear communication. Death is no enemy, not a true loss, nor is it a failure to heal. It is merely the changing of form when the old one is no longer useful for maximal learning. It is nothing to be feared nor longed for. It is merely the doorway to another experience.

60

You Are the Storyteller

"When you maintain that there must be an order of difficulty in miracles, all you mean is that there are some things you would withhold from truth. You believe truth cannot deal with them only because you would keep them from truth."

A Course In Miracles

When you defend your limitations by going into your "story" again it is only because the ego has been threatened by truth. The ego gets activated by any truth which threatens the story the ego tells you. For some it is a story about finances, for some about health, for some about relationships, for others it is about the world . . . the variations go on and on but the purpose of the story is the same in them all—to maintain the belief system the story teaches exactly as it is. In this case, a miracle is the most threatening disturbing thing that can happen and so the ego will attack anyone and anything pointing in the direction of true freedom. The ego is much more comfortable with the seeming "peace" of depression, anger, hopelessness and limitation than with the joy that arises from possibilities. "Quiet desperation" is the ego's idea of peace.

Today, remind yourself frequently that "God is on the field" and that Truth is greater than the "facts" of any story. Remember that a story is changed greatly by tone, editing and intention. The storyteller determines the effect she wants to have by the way she tells the story. When you allow your ego to direct how you will tell the story, it will make you feel worse in the telling. And the more you tell it, the worse you will feel—even if it is only the telling of it in your own mind.

If you MUST tell a story today, tell it in a way that makes you feel better in the telling of it remembering that there is no order of difficultly in miracles. Any story which does not include a miracle is poorly told and poorly edited by the storyteller. And until the miracle happens, the story has not ended.

You are always using your imagination. It is an aspect of consciousness and therefore always active and present. Ego uses imagination to increase Its fortresses of fear and limitation—usually through worry about the future and regret about the past. Your Spirit uses Imagination to reveal the Kingdom of Heaven which exists behind all appearances. Look for the Kingdom today and tell the story of It whether the story is about the past, present or future. God is on the field of Consciousness today. You are not alone. Imagine doors opening for you today. Imagine people are happy to see you when you arrive. Imagine your body is restoring and maintaining perfect balance. Imagine ideal opportunities knocking on your door today. Imagine your heart opening to constant giving and receiving of love. Imagine all necessary resources effortlessly finding you. Imagine yourself telling your friends and loved ones about this wonderful day of effortless joyful miracles. Make that your story and then stick with it.

61

"It's not fair!!! That's not right!!!"

"The ego does not know what it wants to come of the situation. It is aware of what it does not want, but only that. It has no positive goal at all. Without a clear-cut, positive goal, set at the outset, the situation just seems to happen, and makes no sense until it has already happened. Then you look back at it, and try to piece together what it must have meant. And you will be wrong."

A Course In Miracles

Please do not be offended by today's lesson, but We need to point out to humans how often you wake up already thinking of WHAT YOU DO NOT WANT to happen that day. In this way you have already made an enemy of the thing that you hope will not happen. Then, you begin strategizing ways to make sure it does not happen when in fact it already IS happening. It already exists as a fully formed event in your mind and it is just a real for you as if it were physically happening at this very moment. It has instantly manifested for you in this moment even if it never happens in the material realm.

So many of your conversations are focused on the unfairness of life as you obsess over the injustices of your world. At these times almost all of your attention is on what you don't or didn't want and what you think should or should not have happened. You are pushing, pushing, pushing against something. And by the laws of creation, you are invoking MORE of that very thing into your awareness. YOU are upsetting yourself more and more with every word you speak. You call it "venting" but it is INVOKING, CREATING AND ATTRACTING.

Instead, We want you to awaken with a POSITIVE GOAL for your day of what you DO WANT to have happen rather than what you DON'T WANT. Watch your conversations with others and with yourself. Notice how quickly it can go negative if you are not vigilant about having a CLEAR-CUT POSITIVE GOAL in your mind.

You see the Universe is completely fair. It mirrors your own consciousness back to you. It does not give you what you deserve, but rather gives you what you've focused on because it is a "scientific" law and equation. It is no respecter of persons nor personalities. It makes no difference how "nice" of a person you are nor how many gold stars you have on your paper. The Universe is totally fair because it only mirrors your own thought right back to you no matter who you are. As you are already well aware, "Ignorance of the law is no excuse."

SO, what are some clear-cut positive goals? To FOCUS entirely on that which you want to INCREASE in your world. To PRAISE rather than complain. To see what is right instead of what's wrong. To lift up rather than to tear down. Clear loving communication given and received. To live in the peace and Grace of God. To be truly Helpful. To accept your inherent Oneness with the Whole. To encourage, exhort and edify others and yourself. To find the good and praise it. To feel and express gratitude. To ENJOY your life and your day. To make the best of things rather than make the worst of things. To seek out and be the witness to what is good, beautiful and holy.

We are here to help you reach these goals. SOFTEN your heart right now and We will join with you in the achieving of these goals. You need not work HARD at it. In fact, we want you to RELAX deeply in order to ALLOW this to happen. We've got this! YOU set the goal and then step back and allow the instructions to come through each moment. You are not MAKING any of this happen. You are merely lining up your Consciousness with the goal you've set. Now, don't switch goals mid-stream and go back to the old way. But if you do, no worries. Few people travel in a straight line on their journey and no matter how off course you may get, We can get you right back on track the moment you remember your destination again. Now, enjoy the ride!

62

THIS is Your Lucky Day!

"All gifts I give my brothers are my own . . . My treasure house is full, and angels watch its open doors that not one gift is lost, and only more are added. Let me come to where my treasures are, and enter in where I am truly welcome and at home, among the gifts that God has given me."

A Course In Miracles

It's time to open your gifts! It is a day of celebration in which you realize that all that you have ever given has been saved for YOU. You are the recipient of every gift that you have ever given and today is the day when you begin to open and use them.

Every kind smile you have ever given, every tender touch, every encouraging word, every meal you have provided, every laugh you have inspired, every nurturing errand, every word or gesture of forgiveness, every need you have filled, and oh so much more have all been put in the treasure house for YOU. Nothing was ever lost or wasted regardless of how the earthly recipient reacted to your giving. Every gift that you gave, God saved and put away in the treasure house, placing Us at the door to lovingly watch over it all so that it would be here for you when you were ready to open the gifts you gave. It's time to open your gifts!

Be a gracious receiver today. Do not get excited and thereby block your capacity to receive. Breathe into the day and go slowly—learn to SAVOR the experience as you marinate in appreciation. Release the idea of "getting" anything and instead, relax into RECEIVING your precious treasure slowly and gently. Each moment of the day will hold gifts for you if you have eyes to see and ears to hear. If you get in a hurry or become distracted, you will miss the gifts as you go rushing by them.

It turns out that all the gifts you gave in the past were investments that have been in the treasure house accruing interest. See all those kind smiles you gave in the past now being reflected back to YOU today on the faces of those you encounter. Hear those encouraging words you spoke echoing back in your own mind. Feel the cleansing waters of the forgiveness you gave washing over you reflecting your restored innocence and purity.

And from this moment on, you will never fail to know that all that you give is given to yourself. As you give affection, love, admiration and appreciation to others today, you will KNOW that it is all going directly into your own treasure house. You are sacrificing NOTHING today in your giving as you remember and prove that you cannot out give God and you cannot out give yourself.

63

Sweetness Counts

"This day, my Father, would I spend with You, as You have chosen all my days should be . . . This day will be Your sweet reminder to remember You. Your gracious calling to Your holy child, the sign Your grace has come to me, and that it is Your Will I be set free today."

A Course In Miracles

Everything is for your own sake. Every Principle, Law and Instruction is given to you FOR you—to increase your joy, peace, happiness and good. This is why His Course is one without sacrifice. How can there be sacrifice if ALL that you ever do is ultimately for your own greater good?

The forgiveness you give is not for the other person, it is for yourself. Your thoughts never leave your mind. Ideas do not leave their source. Your unforgiveness only crucifies YOU. When you lash out at others, you are lashing out at yourself. When you judge others you judge yourself. When you withhold from others, you withhold from yourself.

This is why you are asked to walk in obedience to Law—for the sake of your own greater good and to avoid suffering. There is no punishment for disobedience whatsoever. There is only cause and effect. What you think and do, is done to yourself. So simple.

As you stay closer to God in your thoughts throughout the day, more and more you will walk in His Love and peace. There is a sweetness that begins to take root in you as you continue to practice walking with Him. The Christ is your Infinite Friend—She will guide and uplift you to the degree that you include Her in your day rather than trying to do everything on your own. Christ is the great Mother/Father, Sister/Brother Who KNOWS the Answer to everything that will confront you today. The word "Christ" means "the anointed one"—and that is you. The Anointed Consciousness lives within every person—seemingly dormant when you are being advised by the ego, and ACTIVE when you turn to It as your Guide.

The world you walk is in great need of sweet relief today. To the degree that you will allow it, We will guide you specifically today where to direct your kindness. We will prompt you to extend a sweet love to those who will most benefit from it today—and it may be those you have the most resistance to so this is a wonderful day to practice obedience—for your own sake. That sweetness may be quietly listening when you would rather interrupt with your good advice. That sweetness may be giving a genuine compliment to someone who has never had a kind word to say to you. That sweetness may be letting someone else take credit for your good idea because they are living in the nightmare illusion of competition. That sweetness may be NOT pointing out the error your loved one has made yet again—even after you've talked about this so many times. ASK US what sweetness to give—We will Help you. Let Us.

Humility, surrender and obedience are words that the ego HATES and rails against—because it knows that these mental attitudes bring more JOY, peace, freedom and genuine happiness than any other spiritual practice you can do.

64

Joyful Love

*"What better purpose could any relationship have than
to invite the Holy Spirit to enter into it and give it His
Own great gift of rejoicing."*

A Course In Miracles

A spiritual relationship is not one in which two people come together to help one another by endlessly correcting the other, giving advice, pointing out a "better" way to look at things or motivating each other to change. Once again, this is the ego co-opting a holy concept by introducing fear and stress into it so that the real goal is either made impossible or delayed as long as possible.

When you think you know what another person needs, you are in your ego and not seeing clearly. People are brought together as assignments in learning how to joyfully love without judgment or correction. ALL true correction is of God and comes by revelation or inspiration, not by motivation. And revelation and inspiration are born in an environment of radical acceptance and love.

Interestingly enough, the people who immediately worry that this will mean being treated as a "doormat" are those for whom this is actually NOT an issue and this is merely their ego's way of blocking the love through pridefulness. At the same time, those with doormat tendencies never seem to think about this possibility and instead block love by staying in situations which We have been guiding them to leave for quite some time. It's insane. Those who are being beaten or abused, whom We have been urging to leave, do the very unloving thing of staying, which is cruel to themselves and to the other. While those who FEEL abused by someone's habitual lateness, or smoking, or carelessly leaving all the lights on, or not calling enough, or being too lazy or too ambitious, or being too needy, or not being "spiritual" enough are really just making excuses to keep abandoning relationships so that they don't have to grow past their own ridiculous petty judgments by simply taking the advice of "get over yourself." The ego is easily and highly offended while spirit is impossible to offend.

THERE IS SO MUCH LOVE FOR YOU if you will simply release your tendency to try to fix and change and motivate your loved ones whether it is a mate, a child, a parent, a business partner, an employee, a neighbor, an agent or anyone else. As you begin to accept others as they are, you will find it much easier to accept yourself as you are. And REAL CHANGE BEGINS WITH ACCEPTANCE. Resistance is not an agent of change. It is a hardening of the heart and closing of the mind. There is no growth or change possible when this kind of calcification is taking place. People change much more permanently in the presence of love and acceptance.

If you will begin to see the best in people you are literally calling more of it forth. If you will begin to imagine the best FOR people without any attachment, you are also calling that forth. As you are willing to overlook their errors and focus instead on their gifts—not keeping it to yourself but VERBALIZING IT TO THEM FREQUENTLY, you will find that your own mood begins to lighten and your heart begins to soften. When you stop waiting for them to change and simply focus on changing your own attitudes and focus, you will find that love becomes joyful and your relationships become happy and serene.

65

The Happy Dream

"The opposite of love is fear, but what is all-encompassing can have no opposite. This course can therefore be summed up very simply in this way: Nothing real can be threatened. Nothing unreal exists. Herein lies the peace of God."

A Course In Miracles

Not everything that goes by the name of love is love. In your world you take the word love so seriously—and the more seriously you take it, the farther from love you actually are. In fact, the physical expression that is truly THE expression of love is laughter. The more laughter, the more love. The more love, the more laughter. Remember, the Course teaches that "to heal is to make happy."

Yet, if We told you to laugh away your problems, you would find that an unreasonable counsel for Us to give you. But that is only because you have made the illusion of opposites real to you. You must remember that there is not God and something else—there is NO opposing force in all the Universe. You must remember that there is not even any such "thing" as an ego. Ego is merely a word used to describe an illusory thought system. It is not a thing and it has no power except in the nightmare.

Laughter and play are signs of the advanced miracle-working Mystic. If you want to move to a new level of mastery, a new level of spiritual advancement, a new level of being truly Helpful, a new level of power to heal . . . bring more laughter and play to your world each day.

66

The Love Strategy

"You are afraid of this because you believe that without the ego, all would be chaos. Yet I assure you that without the ego, all would be love."

A Course In Miracles

As We have told you many times, all strategies are of the ego. They are part of the war on God's reality, the war on inner-peace. And of course, much of your culture is geared toward perpetuating this war and so there is constant and pervasive support in all of your media to keep it going. It has even sunk deep into your New Thought teachings and brought about the insane impossible concept of a "Spiritual Warrior." There is NO SUCH THING AS A SPIRITUAL WARRIOR. That is an extreme oxymoron.

However, We are willing to throw your ego a bone from time to time in order to better train the puppy mind. Since the ego thought system is so constantly hypnotized and mesmerized with the concept of strategies, We will give you a much better oxymoron here to help you taper off the habit of strategizing.

We call it "the Love Strategy." (Of course in reality, it is not a strategy at all but rather a bridging concept for the puppy mind to walk across from the nightmare to the happy dream.)

The Love Strategy is of course, extremely simple because all Truth is simple. In using the Love Strategy, you SIMPLY invoke Divine Love to solve and dissolve every "unsolvable" problem that confronts you. From now on, when a situation arises and you do not know what to do, when fear grips your mind, or when anxiety or depression take hold because of the issue in front of you, and your ego begins the old habit of strategizing on how to "fix" things or to get your needs met, you STOP what you are doing, become still, go inside for a moment and activate "the Love Strategy." The Love Strategy is what you will turn to when you do not know what to do. When you cannot seem to become still enough to receive Guidance, when your normal spiritual routine doesn't seem to be helping, when your ego has become quite activated and you don't even have the energy to clarity of mind to make a sane choice or to DO anything—or perhaps after you've already tried everything else with little or no success, it's time to invoke the Love Strategy.

The Love Strategy is equally applicable if you are working only on yourself, or on an issue, or on a relationship with another person, a government, a company, a judicial system, a financial institution, the economy, a community, a condition or anything else. Rather than trying to conquer your fears, or break through your barriers, or manipulating and controlling, or figuring out exactly what thought pattern or past experience has created this condition, or who is to blame, or what your block is, or trying to force yourself to be courageous, or motivating yourself to take an action of "self-will," or any other such nonsense which merely keeps the war going, you will activate the Love Strategy with your words and thoughts.

The Love Strategy: (the longer version) "DIVINE LOVE IS NOW ACTIVATED AND IS DOING IT'S PERFECT WORK IN EVERY ASPECT OF THIS SITUATION AND WITH EVERYONE INVOLVED. DIVINE LOVE IS DISSOLVING AND NEUTRALIZING ALL THAT IS NOT OF GOD AND OF LIGHT. THE HARD PLACES ARE BEING SOFTENED; PEACE IS REPLACING CHAOS, CLARITY REPLACING CONFUSION. I NOW FULLY AND FREELY RELEASE THIS SITUATION TO DIVINE LOVE TO RESTORE ORDER AND BRING ABOUT THE PERFECT DIVINE SOLUTION AS I NOW TURN MY MIND AND ATTENTION BACK TO GOD. I LET GO OF WHEN AND HOW AND I REST IN GOD."

(the shorter version) *"Divine Love is sorting all of this out for me as I now release the problem to God."*

Then, if at any time you find yourself tempted to give into any form of fear again, remind yourself that the Love Strategy is already at work on this situation and if there is anything for you to do, it will come to you through natural inspiration as We speak right into your heart.

67

Let Us Work It Out FOR You

"It is only because you think that you can run some little part, or deal with certain aspects of your life alone, that the guidance of the Holy Spirit is limited . . . And by so limiting the guidance that you would accept, you are unable to depend on miracles to answer all your problems for you."

A Course In Miracles

If you decide to handle a problem, We step aside and do not interfere in the least. When YOU deal with your problems, you're on your own and are again relying on your own strength. When YOU become the judge of what is appropriate and inappropriate in others and in yourself, We sit back and give you the stage to direct your own drama.

Of course We remain ever in the wings ready to Help and take over in the very moment that you decide that you cannot be your own guide to miracles. The humility that is required to be a miracle worker is greatly resisted by those who insist they KNOW what this situation calls for. And every time you allow your ego to "solve" the problem for you, rest assured that this exact same problem will return over and over and over again in many many forms so that you can make the better choice. The same buttons keep getting pushed until you ask Us to take over and uninstall them for you by surrendering YOUR way to God's Way. Again, the ego's primary problem is a casual daily kind of arrogance.

The endless need of the ego to nurse or share it's wounds and upset "feelings" makes you hostage to what would have been transitory feelings if they had been surrendered to God to purify. And feelings are only the result of the thought system they reflect. You make far far far too much of your hurt injured feelings and are far too easily offended. This IS the cause of ALL war whether between nations or between individuals: pride, arrogance and taking offense. Blessed are the peacemakers who don't have to make sure you know how what you did made them feel the moment they feel it. You can stand up for yourself, or you can let Us stand up for you. The first takes tremendous energy and alertness to the presence of any possible enemy nearing the ego's fortress. The second is a state of effortless Grace, peace and JOY beyond compare.

BUT you cannot merely suppress those feelings and pretend you do not have them and call that holy. You MUST take them to the altar within. You LOOK right at them as you GIVE THEM to the Christ Consciousness within you and ask that your mind be healed. You allow your thoughts to be corrected and healed because THAT is the source of the feelings. Once your mind is corrected, you cease to become a magnet for this particular problem and you have made the necessary progress to move to another level of joyful love and freedom.

> *"You cannot be your guide to miracles, for it is you who made them necessary. And because you did, the means on which you can depend for miracles has been provided for you. God's Son can make no needs his Father will not meet, if he but turn to Him ever so little."*
>
> A Course In Miracles

68

Plan Your Future Good

"A healed mind is relieved of the belief that it must plan, although it cannot know the outcome which is best, the means by which it is achieved, nor how to recognize the problem that the plan is made to solve."

A Course In Miracles

Worry is nothing more than negative planning just as optimism is positive planning. So when We encourage you to plan your future good, we are not talking about a strategy or some self-initiated plan to achieve something or to get something in the world that you think would make you happy.

We are talking about a daily happy optimistic attitude which says *"Only good lies before me and the better it gets, the better it gets."* A healed mind is not micro-managing and planning exactly HOW things will unfold or even necessarily the specifics—it is far too easy for humans to become tormented over this kind of thing and it leaves them in a state of trying to CONTROL things which are none of their business.

Many of you go about life accidentally planning for your decline into old age and all of the horrors you project about that subject—most of it having to do with the serial adventures of the body: will it be sickly, will it be lonely, will it be unattractive, will it have enough money? On and on the mind goes, not knowing that this is planning by default.

So what We are suggesting here is happy planning in which you plan for your continued happiness by visioning yourself as always thriving, always loved, always able, always abundant, always full of JOY and the peace of God. Refuse to entertain any other thoughts. KNOW that We have the perfect plan for all of that already worked out for you and it has been set into motion. There are things for you to do, but We will guide you to them if you will stay in the state of joy and peace. Do not anesthetize yourself with worry or fear or substances but rather awaken to the limitless possibilities for good that are even now planted as seeds for your present and future blessings.

Take some time today to envision the days, weeks, months and years ahead as some of the most joyous of your entire life adventure so far. Be very very general in this visioning and keep most of the focus on YOU, seeing yourself laughing, happy, contented, optimistic, healthy, well taken care of, loved and adored, active and useful, thriving in every way possible. THIS is the kind of happy non-stressful planning which We encourage wholeheartedly because it makes you a vibrational match to good that at this present time you could not even imagine because some of the happy times have to do with things that have not even been invented yet! PLAN being happy, joyous, peaceful and free, but leave the DETAILS of HOW to Us.

69

Revising the Day

*"How can you change the past except in fantasy? . . .
The past is nothing. Do not seek to lay the blame for
deprivation on it, for the past is gone."*

A Course In Miracles

Change a cause, and you automatically change its effects.
How many times have you tossed and turned in bed at night
endlessly obsessing over something that happened that day? And
the obsessing over what happened that day, which is already in
the past, also projects you into terrifying scenarios of what you
think its future effects will be.

So, you are suffering NOW while thinking only about the
past and future, both of which are total fantasy because at this
moment they are happening in mind. Even the past experience
you are ruminating on is seen through the deep and cloudy
filter of the fearful ego mind and is not seen in REALITY.

ALL of this is happening in mind, yet it is sowing the seeds for
your future AND even your present, for it makes physical effects
such as sleeplessness, tension headaches, irritability, stomach acid,

and any number of other phenomenon of the body. And all of this is based on a movie playing IN THE MIND.

So We are counseling you to make a new movie to show. REVISE THE DAY in mind. Go back and see a DIFFERENT PAST—see it in the way that soothes you. Since all mind machinations are fantasy, make a "better" fantasy. Change the cause and you have changed the effects.

Go back in your mind to just before the incident and play it out differently in a NEW fantasy. In the new fantasy, the argument did not happen and only loving words exchanged. We call this "revising the day." In the revision, all hurtful dialogue is replaced with kindness. In the revision the good news came instead of the so-called 'bad" news. In the revision you are the writer, the director, the producer and the actor rather than merely the poor fool whom acts out a bad scene against her will.

Get into it—really FEEL it. Play it over in your mind as if it happened just that way. Play ONLY what feels GOOD to you. Miracles are born from this kind of positive fantasizing and belief. You set a whole new set of effects into action as you practice being diligent about the causes in your life. Keep all of this to yourself—these are techniques of the Urban Mystic which remain within the Secret Societies to be practiced in the way of the Shaman and the Alchemist.

You can practice this at any time of the day or night. We even suggest you put a card on your bed or nightstand that reads, "REVISE THE DAY" so that you will remember this every night as you go to bed. Watch, witness and marvel at the miraculous changes that begin to happen as you consistently re-imagine the causes in your life day by day!

70

Success is a Deliberate Mood

"The Holy Spirit never varies on this point, and so the one mood He engenders is joy. He protects it by rejecting everything that does not foster joy, and so He alone can keep you wholly joyous."

A Course In Miracles

The greatest magnet in the Universe for Law of Attraction to respond to is the vibration of JOY. NOTHING is more dynamically attractive or creates tangible and intangible manifestations more instantly than the vibration of JOY. This is because the Kingdom of Heaven IS JOY itself. So when you are experiencing JOY you are experiencing your authentic Self in your authentic natural habitat, which is the Kingdom.

As you deliberately cultivate a Joyous mood within yourself, you are magnetizing to you the very highest and best in all people, places, things and circumstances. Therefore, whenever you encounter anything that you call a problem, the solution is really NOT about changing the problem—it is about changing your vibration to one of Joy, one way or another.

When you think of health, does the subject stimulate JOY within you? When you think of relationship, does the subject stimulate JOY within you? When you think of career, money, sex, spirituality, home, family, do these subjects stimulate JOY within you? If not, then you know that the ego has managed to infiltrate your thinking and you know where you need to begin to have your thoughts healed.

Begin by allowing the Holy Spirit to guide you to reject every thought that does not foster JOY within you. Remember penguin steps—you are healed one thought at a time. There is no rush in this, but it does require vigilance. BE VIGILANT FOR YOUR JOY! Begin to question every thought which does not inspire JOY within you. Offer them to the Holy Spirit as you begin deliberately CHOOSING thoughts that promote JOY within you. Your vibration can change VERY quickly when you shift to JOY. Start where you are right now.

One way to do this is the "Act As If/Begin With The End In Mind" thinking where you simply jump to a future time in your imagination. SEE, FEEL and EXPERIENCE yourself wholly at peace, joyful and thrilled about the situation that was once your problem even though you don't know HOW it got resolved. As you do this, you are literally creating a new magnetic point of attraction within yourself and are living in the Kingdom. Have FUN with it. Play in imagination as you did when you were a child for you must "become as a little child" if you want to live in the Kingdom today!

71

What Is Given Cannot Be Lost

"How can you who are so holy suffer? All your past except its beauty is gone, and nothing is left but a blessing. I have saved all your kindnesses and every loving thought you ever had. I have purified them of the errors that hid their light, and kept them for you in their own perfect radiance."

A Course In Miracles

So few of you see your past relationships for what they truly are—and because of this you suffer needlessly and build up defenses which merely attract more of the same over and over again with monotonous regularity.

Many of you look at what you gave in past relationships and think that once the form changed or the relationship seemed to end that you lost all that you gave in that relationship. This is yet another of the lies of the ego and one of the ways it steals the joy you could be experiencing.

The Truth is that ALL that you gave in any relationship was given to yourself and you take very bit of it with you wherever you go for all eternity. No kind loving expression was ever wasted no matter the outcome. However, you have free will and are perfectly able to feel deprived and impoverished if you choose to see it that way. You may feel that you wasted years of your life or gave gifts where they were not appreciated or received well. THIS IS YOUR EGO STORY and has nothing whatsoever to do with Truth. In Truth, the more you give, the more you accrue.

Suppose your earthly parents opened a bank account for you when you were born and made weekly deposits all of your life, right up to the present day. But suppose you did not know the account existed? You could think yourself impoverished and lacking. You could tell the story of your poverty as a FACT and BELIEVE every word of it and therefore be totally at the effect of that story. You could die as a millionaire in a shack with dirt floors, never knowing what had been available to you all along.

We are telling you now that you have an Emotional Bank Account in which you have been making deposits of love, kindness, peace, laughter, joy, affection, tenderness, approval, praise, appreciation and all kinds of emotional currency! Every smile you ever gave to another was a deposit into the account and the Christ Consciousness has purified them of all false attachments and any fear which clung to them. You never lose by giving love for every bit of it stays with you for time and all eternity. No one has ever made a fool of you; no one has ever taken advantage of you because what is given can never be lost.

72

Deal With It and Turn It Around

"What fear has hidden is still a part of you. Joining the Atonement is the way out of fear. The Holy Spirit will help you reinterpret everything that you perceive as fearful, and teach you that only what is loving is true."

A Course In Miracles

Fear is like a virus that infects your mental/emotional hard drive. It runs quietly in the background infecting as many files as possible without notice. It infects them with small fear based thoughts that you read in the paper or see on television. It comes from snippets of conversations here and there or from pictures you don't even consciously remember seeing in a magazine. It may come as a faint memory that plays way way in the background, of some thing that was said to you when you were a small child. It can even be a "motivating" slogan which is actually causing you tremendous stress and pressure to perform—something as simple and yet relentlessly stressful as *"living your best life."*

Your system very gradually starts running more slowly, getting more sluggish for seemingly no reason. You feel irritated or lonely from out of nowhere—and yet nothing in your external life has really changed much if at all. Everything just feels different, and not in a good way. Little illnesses and aches and pains start to arise. People are starting to bother you because they breathe too loud. Things seem to feel ovewhelming at times—even simple things and now you start WISHING instead of choosing. Eventually, left unchecked and not dealt with, the small fears will become ovewhelming fears, panic, defensiveness, depression, rage and so much more. It will crash the system.

The ONLY power the fear virus has is that it is HIDDEN and you are not aware of it. It is actually a very weak virus and that is why it must remain hidden—because it is so easily swept away once you are onto it. It is the ONLY virus that exists. There are no others.

You think you are angry, but you are afraid. You think you are depressed, but you are afraid. You think you are impatient, but you are afraid. You think you are frustrated, but you are afraid. You think you are lonely, but you are afraid. You think you are anxious, but you are afraid. You think you have many different problems, but you only have one. The problem is fear.

It is good to do a weekly virus scan. You merely sit down with paper and a pen and go inside to scan for any fears that have come up as you put them down on paper. Write at the top of the page "Virus Scan" and then list whatever uncomfortable thoughts or feelings that you sense within or that appear in mind regardless of what words you use. Don't be spiritual or poetic. Just vomit it all out on paper. Let the ego have it's say on paper where it cannot hurt you or anyone else. Be as petty or judgmental or unspiritual as you feel in that moment. Some weeks there may be a lot—other weeks practically nothing at all.

When you've gotten it out on paper, it's time to move it to the trash file to be deleted. One way to do this is to turn it over to Us as your Cosmic Office Manager to deal with. You may choose to write a prayer of surrendering it all to God: *Dear God, I surrender all these lies of the ego to you to evaporate back into nothingness. I release them to you fully and freely now and am rebooted to my Original Self as You programmed me to be!"*

You can also take those thoughts and turn them around to Prayer Treatment Affirmations. A thought like, *"I'm getting weak and haggard and my body is falling apart"* can become, *"The cells of my body are Divine Intelligence Itself and they know what to do to renew and revitalize themselves each day. Spirit runs my body and I bless my body with love and appreciation."* A fear thought like, *"I'm afraid my savings are going to run out and I'm going to end up losing everything and living on the streets"* can become, *"God is my refuge and security and God goes with me everywhere I go. I am safe and I have Divine Wisdom guiding me to right thought and right actions. Life loves me and I know that doors are opening now for my increased good in all aspects of living."*

If you just take this little once-a-week action to deal with any hidden thoughts or secret beliefs that have crept into your mind, you will find that it SAVES you tremendous time each and every day because your operating system will be running at optimum efficiency. That is what the Atonement is for—it is the ultimate virus scan that detects and wipes clean any corrupted files and puts them back to factory settings of the perfect Child of God.

Don't make a big deal out of this process. Pay MUCH MORE attention to your daily affirmative prayers, spiritual reading, doing lists of positive aspects, gratitude lists, words of praise, savoring and expecting only good. But it is a very good idea to take time at least once a week, for even 10 minutes, to do virus scan to see if any resentments, grievances, guilt, shame, anger, attack and such have crept into your mind so that you can easily sweep them out with the Atonement Program Fear Virus Scanning System. It is only what you keep hidden from yourself that can really hurt you because you've made it inaccessible to the Atonement Principle. Get it up and out quickly and move onto enJOYing a life in which you are under no laws but God's.

73

You Can't Do It Alone

"It cannot be that it is hard to do the task that Christ appointed you to do, since it is He Who does it."
A Course In Miracles

You've heard it said that people are never given more than they can handle. This is ridiculous since mental institutions and graveyards are filled with the bodies of those who had more than they could handle in the physical realm. The Truth is that no one has more than God within them can handle.

First of all, everything comes by vibrational matching so no one is ever "given" anything at all. Everything comes through this kinship. Attention is considered an energetic invitation. Yet there are assignments that you took on and accepted when you came here to this illusion as part of the Great Awakening. You deliberately came here to Help during this Celestial Speedup. You came to Help reverse the direction of energies. It is IMPERATIVE that you understand that this is far too big a task for you to do. Of yourself, it will never be accomplished and you will burn yourself out into cinder and ash.

It can ONLY be done THROUGH you as you step back and let the Christic Consciousness lead the way. **Show up, on time, prepared, doing what you said you would do, with a good attitude. The rest is none of your business and cannot be controlled by you.** We are in need of HAPPY teachers, not martyrs. Let the task be happily done THROUGH you each day. Take time to savor the little and big blessings of each day. Count up the kindnesses and not the challenges. Do not keep score of how "successful" you are being in "getting things done" but rather keep reminding yourself that Christ in you is doing a great Work of which you are not even aware most of the time simply by your Presence. Your energy if FAR more important than anything you ever do or say.

It's so simple really—show up, on time, prepared, doing what you said you would do, with a good attitude. That's all—We'll do the rest through you.

74

Enjoying Each Phase

"Let all things be exactly as they are."
A Course In Miracles

If you are going to thrive under any and all circumstances, you must learn how to enjoy each season and phase of your life just as it is and just as it is not. Little children want to be older so they can do this or that. Senior citizens want to be younger so they can do this or that. Humans put up so much resistance to what and where they are at any given time. So little time is spent actually appreciating and enjoying the current phase because there is always some thing, big or small, that is missing or that you wish were not present.

So often you wish you could be up running around when you are in a season of physical healing. When in a season of high activity and running to and fro, you wish you were able to just put your feet up and relax for a whole day on the sofa doing nothing. When funds are too low you are desperately striving to get more and when there is a lot you worry that taxes will take it all away or you are engaged in some legal battle to try to keep it. When you are single you bemoan the fact that there is no one to share your life with. When you are in relationships you complain of a lack of privacy or "me" time and feel overwhelmed by the needs of others. All of this leaves you with about 45 minutes in your whole waking lifetime between physical birth and death when you actually feel truly contented. We won't even bother going into the HUGE issues you have wasting time wanting your bodies to be different than they are.

Remember that "hell is what the ego has made of the present"—and this is accomplished through your thoughts and attitudes about this very moment exactly as it is. When you learn to make the BEST of things rather than making the worst of them, your life is full of beautiful moments every single day. But you cannot notice the beautiful moments when your attention is forever on CHANGING what is and wishing it were different. There is a time for reaping and a time for sowing. There is a time for great activity and a time for rest and reflection. For everything there is a time and a purpose.

Welcome what today has to offer you. Let go of what you think "should" be happening or "shouldn't" be happening to meet today just as it is. Then, see what you can make of it. How can you make the very best of THIS day just as it is and just as it is not? What is there to bless and be grateful for? Make friends with the circumstances of your life today instead of enemies and watch how many beautiful moments rise up to meet you—one after another after another after another.

75

Let Your Light So Shine

> "The holy relationship, a major step toward the perception of the real world, is learned. It is the old, unholy relationship, transformed and seen anew."
>
> A Course In Miracles

As you walk farther and farther in the Light, it will become increasingly difficult to hide your joy in this world of sadness and pain. It can at times be as extreme as a scene from one of your movies, "The Invasion of the Body Snatchers" in which the dark emotionless pod people who walk as the dead see immediately that you are not one of them.

That Light is IN you and it is your Salvation from the illusory pain and sadness that this world projects and promotes. Your smile will seem loony to those who still walk the world asleep—a betrayal of the agreement for darkness. You were born with that Light in you, but the ego systems trained it out of you bit by bit. The smiling laughing joy of babies shows you your natural state. And in your modern age, you can see that at younger and younger ages your children develop the ego's false tough persona. Smiling is not cool and so a tough sneer of arrogance is cultivated.

Most of the musicians of your world project a deeply unhappy image—look at their photos and you would think that music was a form of torture. Everything in your world is upside down and validates the unholy relationship of fear, pain and suffering within the illusion. You even "work" on your relationships. Your language itself is geared toward making sure no joy or Light seeps in to make you seem silly or not to be taken seriously.

So, We are warning you, if you continue walking with Us, there will come a time when you can no longer hide your smile, your joy, your Light. More and more you will SEE the world differently and be less and less tempted to fall into the trap of taking illusions seriously. You will see beyond the masks and disguises of those who are trying to "fix" the world or who are trying to get from the world what they think they need. And you will see that your sight has been transformed into VISION. The world has not changed, YOU have changed. You have reverted to using the vision of a child. Oh what miracles you will behold in a world of magic, love and miracles which have ALWAYS surrounded you.

You are a Lighthouse—a beacon in a storm. Others will find you. If this is not what you wanted—best to get out now and hurry back to the nightmare before it's too late.

76

No Bitching Allowed

"Each grievance you hold is a declaration, and an assertion in which you believe, that says, "If this were different, I would be saved." The change of mind necessary for salvation is thus demanded of everyone and everything except yourself."

A Course In Miracles

Most of you have no idea at all how much time you spend bitching, whining and complaining. Shockingly enough, the more comfortable your life is, the greater your propensity for this kind of behavior. We hear this from humans all the time and it is victim mentality at it's worst. At this level of consciousness you can be as miserable living in a castle with servants as living in a cardboard box under a freeway.

And you live by the laws of whatever kingdom of consciousness you are dwelling in. Victim consciousness is about not taking responsibility for you own moods and attitudes. It is looking to the world and others to feather your nest and make you more comfortable every moment.

"The room is too cold, my chair is uncomfortable, this clerk is too slow, they should fix the economy, my mate should be kinder to me, they need to learn to park, people need to be more respectful, good help is impossible to find, my supervisor ought to appreciate me more, customer service is non-existent these days, the neighbors should clean up their yard!" All of these are grievances which assert that OTHERS need to change so that the ego can be happy. But even if the whole world bowed down and made every change necessary, the ego is INCAPABLE of happiness for more than fleeting moments.

"They should do something about this. I'm going to make a suggestion." This is the mantra of victim consciousness. Victims think that making suggestions IS doing something when all it does is reaffirm that others are responsible for making you happy and contented.

Thriving under any and all circumstances means exactly what it says. And because the you get what you focus on, as you move from bitching and complaining to praising and appreciating, you will find that the better it gets, the better it gets.

77

ASK and LISTEN

"You are not misguided, you have accepted no guide at all. Instruction in perception is your great need, for you understand nothing. Recognize this but do not accept it, for understanding is your inheritance. Perceptions are learned, and you are not without a Teacher. Yet your willingness to learn of Him depends on your willingness to question everything you learned of yourself, for you who learned amiss should not be your own teacher."

A Course In Miracles

The problem that far too many spiritual types have is asking for help but not for guidance. Because you have diagnosed the problem yourself (and you are wrong) you ask for help in solving or healing it. You would do far better instead to ASK for guidance and information FIRST and THEN LISTEN for the Answer. We are the League of Angels! As you know, Angels are the messengers of God. We have SO MUCH to tell you—but you so rarely ASK or LISTEN.

Much of the time you make a plan based on YOUR idea of what the problem is and then use enormous amounts of your psychic mental emotional and physical energy trying to get that plan to come to fruition. Often you are wasting your true Creative Powers this way. It would be so much easier if you would ASK instead, *"What do I need to know about this situation? What is my REAL need here? What would You have me do, think, say? What am I to learn from this? What is the REAL problem?"*

Then RELAX and DEEPLY LISTEN for the Answers to come. Close your eyes, breathe, GO DEEP INSIDE where We speak to you—leave the realm of your head where you are trying to FIGURE it all out—go down into your belly past the emotional attachments and sentimentality of the heart. The gut is where We speak to your through your intuition—your "gut" feelings. You need not "feel" something there but We are telling you this as an imaging process to get you out of the mental FIXING energy that mostly kicks up confusion.

Mental energy is a wonderful gift of God when it is in service to the Spirit that is you. We also want you to leave the heart center because too often what you think of as love is really egoic attachment and are weak victim consciousness vibrations that you learned from misguided spiritual precepts which were more about sacrifice and pain than about the FIERCE vibration that is LOVE! The heart is a wonderful servant to the Spirit that is you, but it is a terrible leader. DO NOT follow your heart! Follow your gut—that is the place of connection to Source. Then let your heart and head follow THAT Guidance.

Again, ASK and LISTEN. Things will go so much more smoothly and without all the drama, worry, stress and fear. We have so much to give you and want only the very highest and best for you. Help Us help you.

78

Consciousness Animates Matter

"Only what you have not given can be lacking in any situation."

A Course In Miracles

Of course it is quite obvious to you that Consciousness animates matter since what you call death is such an extreme example of how matter decays as soon as you've left the building. The simple fact is, you live in a "use it or lose it" world. This applies to all of life and all physical manifestation.

Even your relationships begin to decline the moment your focus and attention are withdrawn from them. Every relationship is animated with the consciousness of those in the relationship. And they are animated by the KIND of attention and focus of the consciousnesses. They are infused with the energy of positive aspects or negative aspects, depending on which is focused on. This is also why relationships can be a roller coaster ride for those who do not know how to focus their attention or work with Consciousness.

The roller coaster relationship with money, or a mate, or family, or business associates, or the body and health . . . this is the result of focusing on what IS rather than going beyond appearances to the Source of all Creation. But once a miracle worker has become so sensitive that she is no longer able to tolerate lack of love in herself, she begins to want to feel good more than she wants to be right. THIS is the great turning of the corner at last!

If there is some area of your life which seems dead, it is either because you have begun to withdraw your consciousness from that area without realizing it—perhaps because you don't REALLY want to continue on there, or you are giving it more negative focus and attention than positive. Perhaps you are looking at what you can "get" there rather than what you have to give. This always leads to feeling cheated, depleted and ripped off and once this sets in you MUST shift your vibration or it will only move more steadily toward decay.

In a "use it or lose it" world, one of the most dangerous things you can do is to hoard manna. You live in the most hoarding culture We have ever experienced in all the Universe since the beginning of what you call time. Even your "homeless" burden themselves down with shopping carts full of rotting manna. They are no MORE insane than those of you in houses with overflowing garages of things you do not use. If it is not being used and focused on, there is not enough consciousness animating it to keep it from falling into decay and ash.

And of course CALM RELAXED loving gratitude and appreciation is perhaps the best kind of attention and focus you can give to anything or anyone. Becoming hyper-vigilant and obsessed with something or someone IS negative attention because it is rooted in fear of loss.

Take some time to consider your life as you go through the various aspects, people, places, things, and relationships. Then look to see how your Consciousness is animating or not animating each area. Start where you are. Don't allow yourself to get overwhelmed—miracles happen one thought at a time. Remember, penguin steps.

79

Start Where You Are

"Do not fight yourself. But think about the kind of day you want, and tell yourself there is a way in which this very day can happen just like that. Then try again to have the day you want. The outlook starts with this: Today I will make no decisions by myself."

A Course In Miracles

Do not ever throw a day away. Know that at any moment you are free to start the day all over again from NOW. Now is always where your power resides. Some days it may seem that you have needed to start the day over a dozen times or more. This is totally unimportant. What matters is the willingness to keep making the better choice over and over again.

You may start out with a clear loving intention for the day and find that 30 minutes later it all seems to have disintegrated into chaotic attack thoughts. So what? Begin again right now. REMEMBER your goal and get right back on the highlighted route. Remember there is only ONE failure in all the Universe and that is the failure to learn the lesson in front of you.

Happily enough, you have all of eternity to learn so every failure is TEMPORARY. It's not "now or never" but rather "sooner or later." But remember NOT to be your own teacher for you will vacillate between being overly strict and vicious with yourself, or far too lax and permissive. You often start out in the morning as the strict teacher who is going to have a "perfect" record for the day and then once you make even one mistake, you become defeated and passive and throw away the whole day by not even trying again. The ego lives in absolutes—all or nothing!

But if you turn to your Internal Team you can have a meeting where all decisions are made from the Higher Consciousness. This is what it means to make no decisions by yourself. You are not alone, but you can blind yourself to the Others Who walk with you and cut Them off from your awareness. This is very frightening and lonely for most who attempt this way of living in the world.

There is another way. You can choose to share your life today with Us and with you We can make the decisions that will bring about a day of Grace and ease. Do not count up your errors today or how many times you've had to begin again or the errors of those around you but instead count only your willingness to be a joyful learner. YOU are the only once keeping score of anything anyhow so keep the scores that make you feel good!

80

A Working Vacation

"You are not really capable of being tired, but you are very capable of wearying yourself. The strain of constant judgment is virtually intolerable. It is curious that an ability so debilitating would be so deeply cherished."

A Course In Miracles

It's a wonderful day for you to take a vacation from judgment. Just for today. One day away from judging and evaluating your body, how much money you do or do not have, judging your feelings, judging how your work or career is going or not going, judging your romantic partner or lack of one, judging the people behind the counter and in line, judging any and all progress today, judging the weather and the traffic, judging your daughter's addiction, judging your mother's dementia and your brother's drinking. TAKE A VACATION DAY right in the middle of your normal daily activities.

Let your mind rest from sizing things up—just for one day. Let it all go as if you were gently floating on a raft in the pristine clear waters at the most relaxing private resort in the world far far from everything you know. Keep this as your mental atmosphere even right in the middle of a day that may be the extreme opposite of that.

And what if you need to make some "judgment calls" today? What if that is part of your "job" and is required of you? What if you need to make decisions for your children or your committee? No worries. You can look right at the data, the information, and the options and respond directly from your Center—without judgment or confusion. Every Answer is inside you and without judgment you will find that it is even EASIER to locate those Answers—without drama, confusion, and without defensiveness. Clarity and Guidance comes much more quickly and effortlessly without the strain of judgment.

Take just one day away from it—see how it goes. Then, if you choose, you may want to extend it indefinitely.

81

A World of Wonder

*"Watch with me, angels, watch with me today. Let all
God's holy Thoughts surround me, and be still with me
while Heaven's Son is born . . . Let Christ be welcomed
where He is at home."*

A Course In Miracles

The Holy Christ is born over and over and over again
millions and billions of times every day through an act of
recognition and acceptance. The anointed Consciousness,
which is what Christ is, is activated through this witnessing. It
is the seed of miraculous potentiality within every person, place
and situation in your world today. It in no way intrudes but it
is ever available for those who will drop judgment for even a
moment—just long enough to use a different kind of seeing.

Today you can behold a world of pain, suffering, struggle
and limitation . . . or you can activate the World of Wonder.
Let Us Help you. You are used to SEEKING and FORCING
but this is NOT the path to the miracles that can touch you
today. You will need to relax your natural tendency to RESIST

anything that does not fit your pictures of the perfectly ordered day. You will need to soften your gaze and accept that you do not always perceive a miracle when it is right in front of you. You often do not see the forest for the trees.

When you feel your resistance to a person or a situation rise up today, STOP in that very moment and realize the door to the World of Wonder is right before you hidden behind the mists which the ego has put up in your awareness. DO NOT BLOCK YOUR BLESSING but instead ACTIVATE YOUR BLESSING by blessing the person or situation in front of you! The blessing you withhold keeps you lost in the fog. The blessing you give opens the gates to the World of Wonder. Give kindness rather than correction. Give warmth rather than the cold shoulder. Give patience rather than a sharp word.

Make no distinction or separation in this. That means that you include yourself as you would any other person or situation. If some aspect of yourself or your life arises in your awareness—again, let go of resisting and move into the awareness that the Christ seed within you will be activated by your willingness to recognize and accept it in yourself even when there is no evidence of it whatsoever at the moment.

We will Help you. This has the potential to be quite an amazing day if you will help Us Help you.

82

Love The One You're With

"The ego is certain that love is dangerous, and this is always its central teaching. It never puts it this way; on the contrary, everyone who believes that the ego is salvation seems to be intensely engaged in the search for love. Yet the ego, though encouraging the search for love very actively, makes one proviso; do not find it. Its dictates, then, can be summed up simply as: 'Seek and do not find.' This is the one promise the ego holds out to you, and the one promise it will keep. For the ego pursues its goal with fanatic insistence, and its judgment, though severely impaired, is completely consistent."

A Course In Miracles

CALL OFF THE SEARCH! Bring in the dogs. Send everyone home. YOU are the one you've been seeking after. The love that you want has always been right here, right now. The search was itself a way to avoid this realization. You left home in order to find what can only be found at home. This is the theme in story after story in your world. Everyone who leaves home in search of treasure returns home to where the search began to find true completion of the journey. There is nothing "out there" to find.

For all eternity you will be with you. There is no escaping your Self. There is only distraction and delay. This is wonderful news and as you begin to embrace it, it will bring a joy and peace that knows no limit. The love and acceptance of Self is not an exclusive love, but an inclusive love. You need not worry that the end of your search for love will mean loneliness and isolation—quite the contrary. When you are finally AT HOME with yourself, you will find an endless knocking at your door by those who've come to share their love with you.

When the searching is over, the finding has begun at last.

Begin by dropping all attack thoughts about yourself—ALL of them. Keep none of them—not even the "reasonable" ones. Begin from this moment on treating yourself as the most beloved mate, child, friend you have ever dreamed of having. THIS is the divine romance with Self. Look in the mirror each morning and say, *"Morning sunshine, I'm so glad we're going to spend the day together! Let's have our best day ever so far! I'm going to take good care of you today and we're going to share our Light with anyone who shows up on the pathway today! The better it gets, the better it gets!"*

NOTHING is more attractive than a joyful, loving, fully whole person. And since like attracts like, your Light will draw to you those who are also joyful, loving and fully whole. No more searching—only finding and having.

83

Praying For Others

"What you acknowledge in your brother you are acknowledging in yourself, and what you share you strengthen."

A Course In Miracles

We want to counsel you to begin to be much less casual in your conversation in order to be far more deliberate. You make many more errors in "casual" conversation than you do in the "big" errors that you tend to focus on and regret in your daily curriculum.

For a time it would be good for you to think of all conversation, including those which are written, as an affirmative prayer treatment, because it actually is just that. Therefore, notice whether what you are doing a blessing or a cursing of that which you are discussing. You are FAR TOO CASUAL ABOUT YOUR WORDS when you describe the people, places and things of your life and world. You do not realize that you are creating a cause—and every cause has an effect.

In every conversation that you have about another person, you are making an affirmative prayer. You either loose her, or bind her free by your words. And if you jail her with your words, you will be the jailer who sits next to her IN A JAIL which you constructed with your words.

Perhaps you think you are merely describing the facts of a situation. Most likely this is a justification and a lie. A description is this: *"My brother is in a hospital bed 24 hours a day now."* Period. An affirmative prayer treatment is this: *"My brother is a severe alcoholic whose done so much damage to himself that he is dying. His children are all messed up because of all the years of alcohol abuse and now it's all a huge mess and drama. We've tried to help him for years but he has messed up every chance he's been given because he has always been the baby and never takes responsibility for himself."* THAT IS A PRAYER TREATMENT and a CAUSE which YOU are aligning with, thereby setting LAW into action.

Not only that, but YOU are at the effect of that prayer. It activates FEELINGS in you as well as a whole litany of bio-chemical reactions in your body vessel. When you LABEL people as dysfunctional, aggressive, chronically late, irresponsible, full of toxic anger, self-obsessed, temperamental, greedy, and so on—THOSE ARE AFFIRMATIVE PRAYER TREATMENTS. They are not mere observations—they set LAW into motion and YOU are at the effect of the laws you set into motion.

Try to remember, *"I don't know what anything, including this, means."* Begin to DELIBERATELY speak words of power into every conversation. DELIBERATELY PRAY in your "casual" conversation about everyone and everything. *"My brother is in a hospital bed 24 hours a day now and we've consulted a Higher*

Authority because lots can happen. We believe in an Infinite Spirit of restoration and renewal. Whatever happens we know that all things are held perfectly in the hands of God."

INVOKE and activate the best in everything and everyone by your casual conversation. With your boss, your annoying co-worker, your out of control children, the mate who "never" listens, the parent who withholds approval, the neighbor who is lazy and passive, the ignorant political figure who is ruining the country, the manager who isn't doing enough for your career, the local government which is ruining your city, the entitled spoiled celebrity who has no appreciation for endless chances she's had—all of those descriptions that you casually think to yourself or say to others can be changed from words of negative power to words of positive power. And YOU will be at the effect of what you acknowledge in others so make it good!

You must IMAGINE the good into being rather than becoming mesmerized by what IS and has been! You need not be specific either. You can be extremely general as We were in the prayer treatment above. HOW is not your part, WHAT is your part.

84

Appreciate and Savor Your Way In

"Try then, today, to begin to learn how to look on all things with love, appreciation and open-mindedness. You do not see them now. Would you know what is in them? Nothing is as it appears to you. Its holy purpose stands beyond your little range. When vision has shown you the holiness that lights up the world, you will understand today's ideas perfectly. And you will not understand how you could ever have found it difficult."

A Course In Miracles

Joy in your world is largely contingent on your ability to appreciate and savor whatever is the object of your attention at any given moment. You find this easy when something is shiny and new to you, but the longer your exposure, the easier it is to take it for granted as you gradually begin to let your attention drift to darker thoughts.

We will remind you again that babies are a perfect example of this lesson. Most people find it easier to stay focused on savoring and appreciating small children because they are constantly changing. As they grow, you are delighted with the new thing they are learning and the surprising way they look at life. They keep your attention and interest because you don't grow bored with them and therefore you do not take them for granted. You give them a tremendously long "period of grace" in which you are loving them and flooding them with positive attention even when they are making thousands of mistakes and messing up all your well-laid plans. It is not until they reach their teenage years that you begin to find their changes less that delightful and surprising. At that point it takes more discipline to feel ONLY joy when they are the object of your attention.

With adults it is not so easy for you because once the initial period of newness wears off it is much easier to stop focusing on the positive aspects through your appreciation of them and you begin to let your mind drift to their "faults." As you spend less time savoring and appreciating them as they are, you find that your own joy begins to diminish. You will find that you have been ejected from the Kingdom by your own attention to the things that are not a mental equivalent to the JOY, peace and love of the Kingdom.

But there is a way back in—savor and appreciate your way back in! When you grow bored with your job or begin to feel trapped by it, start to find little things to savor and appreciate in your work environment and give that as much of your attention as possible. If at times your body seems to you to be too this or not enough that, when there is the presence of "dis-ease" of some sort, look for aspects of the body that you can savor and appreciate just as it is and magnify that in your awareness and conversation as much as possible. If you feel stuck in a boring rut and everything around you seems lackluster, routine and shabby, grab hold of your thoughts and begin directing them to savoring and appreciating one or two little things and then spend as much time as possible giving those things your full attention. If a relationship seems like it has gotten stale and boring, or you've begin to be greatly annoyed with all the little things that the other person does or fails to do which are enraging or depressing you, begin to make daily lists of all the wonderful little things there are to appreciate and savor about him or her.

The ego tells you that your joy, peace and love are contingent on having a life which constantly inspires those emotions in you. But We are telling you that is the way the ego keeps you unhappy and ever searching for what it refuses to let you find as it leads you down one dark blind alley after another. You must have noticed that ego's "happiness" always has a very short shelf life and is extremely shaky at best.

Make the effort today to breathe new life into your life through the practice of savoring and appreciating. SLOW DOWN your racing mind throughout the day to really SEE what is in front of you. What or who have you been taking for granted? Do you daily appreciate the physical vehicle you call your body? Do you savor the mattress you sleep on each night? As the water from your shower rains down upon you do you realize what an opulent blessing it is that you are able to live in such luxury which very few humans experienced just a few generations ago? As you drive your car or take public transportation, speeding along the paved roads, do you understand that your ancestors would have taken many hours to make a journey that you make in minutes?

We so want to spoil and pamper you every day of your life, but We also want you to never lose your ability to savor and appreciate every bit of it because if you don't, YOU will find yourself bored, agitated and depressed even while all your dreams are coming true. We want to pamper you so that you can be a JOYful teacher of love helping in this time of the Celestial Speedup. Take none of it for granted and you will be exactly that! Savor and appreciate your way to JOY today. We have many wonderful things to accomplish through you and the happier you are, the easier it is for Us to use you.

85

You Are Not Alone

"Truth has rushed to meet you since you called upon it. If you knew Who walks beside you on the way that you have chosen, fear would be impossible."

A Course In Miracles

Throughout these lessons We have regularly reminded you of this fact. You are not alone. You are not alone. You are not alone. Are you understanding this? Are you allowing this in—truly?

Whatever lies before you today, you are not alone. We are here. God is here. There is no separation and no distance except in illusions.

Every moment of every day Spirits surround you and watch over you. You need only shift your attention to the world just beyond the veil by simply knowing that it IS. With this awareness you can drop your story. With this you will find the peace of God. With this there is nothing to fear.

You are not alone. You are not alone. You are not alone.

We will join you in all that you have to do today. We will Help you if and when you ask. We WANT to Help you. We WANT to Help you enjoy this day. We are here. You are not alone.

86

Micromanaging the Meaningless

"You still have too much faith in the body as a source of strength . . . It is impossible to accept the holy instant without reservation unless, just for an instant, you are willing to see no past or future . . . when the light comes at last into the mind given to contemplation; or when the goal is finally achieved by anyone, it always comes with just one happy realization, 'I need do nothing.'"

A Course In Miracles

To say that you have too much faith in the body as a source of strength means the ways that you believe your mental machinations will "save" you from present and future catastrophe or even discomfort. Your faith in the mind and its plans to defend against loss is costing you the peace that is your natural inheritance. You still spend too much time micromanaging the meaningless. So often you are looking at all the wrong things and tormenting yourself needlessly.

Relax miracle worker. You cannot think or DO your way to peace and safety. You cannot *"stay on top of things"* enough to get or maintain your physical world in the perfection that you THINK will bring you security, peace and joy. Peace and joy are right here, right now. STOP and breathe in the peace and power of this moment. Drop all your strategies which are merely hopeless defenses against imagined future chaos. Let go of the future and place it in the hands of God where it belongs. It does not exist at all except in some story you tell to motivate or terrify yourself. Let it go. Today's sufficiency is here. Remember, when it comes to your life and "problems," We've got this.

The word We want you to focus on is "need." I NEED do nothing. Of course you will do things because doing can be quite joyous. Right this moment you are reading, which is a doing. It's the word NEED that gets your ego activated. There is a monologue going on in your minds much of the time which is all about *"I have to, I need to, I should, I should have . . ."* which is creating tremendous pressure on you and it sucks the joy out of your present moments. It is a cruel form of self-motivation and punishment.

Change the monologue to a dialogue with Source. Let the cruel motivations become Our gentle inspirations. It will sound more like, *"I want to, I get to, I love to . . ."* Place your present and future in the hands of God today little miracle worker. Let go of micromanaging and allow Us to guide you one penguin step at a time deeper and deeper into the peace and joy within you and watch how many miracles happen without even trying.

87

Go Within

"Simply do this: Be still, and lay aside all thoughts of what you are and what God is; all concepts you have learned about the world; all images you hold about yourself. Empty your mind of everything it thinks is either true or false, or good or bad, of every thought it judges worthy, and all the ideas of which it is ashamed. Hold onto nothing. Do not bring with you one thought the past has taught, nor one belief you ever learned before from anything. Forget this world, forget this course, and come with wholly empty hands unto your God."

A Course In Miracles

Much of the time your ego thought system is founded on the scarcity principle in which it always seems that something is missing. We call this the Magpie Mentality. It is the tendency to spend your days gathering up, gathering up, gathering up endless bits and pieces of information that amounts to nothing more than shiny tin foil. This mind is so FULL of ideas and concepts and wants and desires. It is so very hungry and yet it is already bursting at the seams. There is very little breathing space or places to rest.

Remember that miracles undo. They are a letting go and a release. Miracles are an emptying out of all the meaningless "treasures" that the ego continues to stockpile and hoard. Remember too that what is full cannot be contributed to. The mind that thinks it knows cannot be taught.

Thriving is not about HAVING the most or even in having everything happen the way you think it should happen, nor when or with who. Thriving is the recognition of your sufficiency in this very moment. God is your sufficiency in all things and at all times. Yes, even in *this*, whatever this happens to be at the moment.

So just for now, let go of trying to figure out your day, or your life, or the life of another. Become still, go inside and create some space. What is it time for you to release to Spirit? What is it time to let go of? What old limiting beliefs, attachments, regrets, addictions, demands, stories, grievances, conditions, behaviors, yearnings, negative thoughts, resentments and fears is it time for you to let go of? It is impossible to "get rid of" any of them, but it is totally possible to release them to Spirit as you gently lay them on the altar within as the only "sacrifice" you are ever asked to make—the sacrifice of what does not serve Who you really are. It is the releasing of all guilt, shame and blame.

This is a sacred day of freedom and adventure for you! As you empty yourself out in the Sanctuary Within, you are then actually open to receive the gifts We have for you. You have no idea the wonderful miracles that will fill your life until you begin this daily emptying out of yesterday's manna. You are the priestess, the priest, here in your temple garments to be washed clean in the Living Waters of the Font to prepare you for entering the world fresh and new each day. Come here any time—morning, noon or night. We are always here ready to serve you as you release whatever has been gathered up in the world of illusions and to remind you again of how simple Salvation really is because there is nothing to be saved from except the anxiety and despair of a mind full of complicated erroneous concepts and ideas.

We are here for you. And We love you. We love you. We love you.

88

Revise the Script

"There is no point in lamenting the world. There is no point in trying to change the world. It is incapable of change because it is merely an effect. But there is indeed a point in changing your thoughts about the world. Here you are changing the cause. The effect will change automatically."

A Course In Miracles

Our great and brilliant Brother Neville taught his students to use the "pruning shears of revision" on the nightmare aspects of their day. We agree that this is indeed a powerful creative tool when used correctly. It is a very simple process which can be done at any time, but it is particularly helpful in those moments just before drifting off to sleep.

You are always projecting your version of your life onto a mental screen in which you are of course, the central character. And many of you torment yourself at the end of the day by going over and over the most disturbing parts of your day. You watch and ruminate on those scenes over and over again, going in quite close on the most upsetting parts and then fearfully projecting more scenes of what might happen in tomorrow's shooting schedule.

But you can revise the script even after it's been shot. Remember, miracles are also retroactive. Time and space are illusions within the dream that you call reality. Therefore, it can be quite beneficial for you to revise whatever happened in your mind until you feel more peaceful and in alignment with Source. When you mentally change a cause, you have automatically changed the effects of that cause based largely on the strength of your faith and belief. ALL things are possible as long as you remain perfectly in alignment with God and are NON-ATTACHED to the outcome as possible.

This is not an egoic fear-based negative kind of denial or suppressing of information at all. It is a positive activation of the Christ Consciousness. In this revision, you replay the scene in which the argument occurred and this time you see peaceful encouraging communication given and received. You replay the scene in which you were given the disturbing diagnosis and this time you rewrite the dialogue in whatever soothing way your Higher Self directs. Do it for as long as it takes to begin to feel more calm and centered. Allow yourself to drift off to sleep seeing the new improved movie. Do this as many nights (and even at times during the day) as it takes to keep you centered in your Holy Self.

And then each day, go about your life dealing with life as your Guides direct. You may still be directed to looking for a new job, or having your medical treatments, or apologizing to your mate, or making arrangements to pay off the debt. In fact, the disturbing event may very well have been a necessary step in moving you along to something which is going to be much better for you. But in the meantime, the revision process can be helpful in moving your vibration back into alignment with Truth.

Every cause has an effect that reflects the nature of the cause. If YOU change the cause within yourself mentally, you change the effects that YOU will experience. PLAY with this idea. Make it enjoyable. Experience it for yourself. It is a very effective and enjoyable tool in your spiritual tool kit which is best when used frequently.

89

Help Us Help You

"Ask Him very specifically: What would You have me do? Where would You have me go? What would You have me say, and to whom? Give Him the rest of the practice period, and let Him tell you what needs to be done by you in His plan for salvation. He will answer in proportion to your willingness to listen. This is enough to establish your claim to God's answer."

A Course In Miracles

Are you worn down and exhausted from all the fighting yet? Oh, We understand that you are a "spiritual" type and rarely get into dramatic verbal arguments anymore. We're talking about all the fighting you do with the television news, on the Internet, in the car, and in your own mind as you engage in imaginary fights with those who are not even in the room with you. We know that it really can be very exciting and gets your energy going—before it crashes you down into hopelessness and despair.

You want so much to be a positive force of good on the planet and to those you love. We know how much you want to help end the suffering on the planet. We know how vigilant you can be at times about this. Yet you do not realize how frequently you are allowing the ego to be your "guide" to miracles and healing. If you did, you would drop this self-defeating habit and awaken to Reality again.

What is tragically amusing are the "religious" fights that dominate the planet and even dominate your own mind as you defend against those you feel attacked you with their sacred books. Of course, in your mind this defense is justified because "they started it." Those who are Thrivers have dropped the "they started it" mentality and so must you if you want to BE the truly Helpful miracle worker that We know you to be. Attacking or defending against a religion because you feel attacked by it? Hopeless.

The problem is still very simple. You forget to ASK Him FIRST. You REACT and then pray about it later. This wastes time. Remember that miracles are a means of SAVING time. But too often you think that you are wasting time if you stop to ASK within rather than responding immediately to the perceived "attack." And honestly, many of you very easily feel attacked. A question as simple as, "where were you?" can send you running for your shield and armor. This is how the ego steals your peace and keeps you from fulfilling your miracle working function. This is most important in your personal interactions with others. In fact, you can be the laziest when it comes to communication with those you love the most. You speak first and think later. This can be very harmful since the ego speaks first and speaks loudest.

STOP defending and begin creating. Stop endlessly looking things up in spiritual books and spend more time communing with the Mother Father Creator within. Stop fighting against the darkness and spend more time turning on the Light of your Divine Consciousness.

It's so simple that it is difficult for many of you to believe. If every sacred book in the world were destroyed there would be a brief span of physical time in which humans would once again turn to the Presence within for Guidance and peace would ripple out across the land. But within a VERY SHORT period of time, far less than even one generation, those truths would begin to be organized into belief systems and the ego would use them to attack and defend. Therefore, make no enemy of any book or spiritual group and do not fight against them. Instead, ASK God to Guide you today very specifically in all things. As the Course teaches, "You are never bereft of Help, and Help that KNOWS the Answer."

The real Answer has NOTHING to do with getting rid of your problems, or enemies or diseases, or anything. It has to do with turning entirely away from your obsession with problems and turning entirely in the direction of the Answer, which is always your connection to God within.

90

The Love Solution

"Be not afraid of love. For it alone can heal all sorrow, wipe away all tears, and gently waken from his dream of pain the Son whom God acknowledges as His."

A Course In Miracles

Simply put, all anyone wants is to be adored, to be noticed, to be seen, known and understood. If that does not seem to be available, many people will settle for negative attention in order to feel the hit of energy that comes from any attention at all. Therefore all attention is a kind of reinforcement. What you give attention to, and the kind of attention you give, is a powerful activating combination.

When you give great negative attention to something you dislike in another person, they will unconsciously begin giving you MORE of that very thing. When you give great positive attention to something you love in another person, they will unconsciously begin giving you MORE of that very thing. Attention invokes. When you yell at your dog for barking, the dog hates the yelling but loves the energy hit and you are in effect training her to bark

MORE so she can feel the energy hit from you, her beloved. Billions of people react the same way as the domesticated dog.

Therefore, if you become one who walks the earth scattering positive energy on people for everything you see in them worth celebrating and acknowledging, you are invoking the very best from all people and situations. People blossom in the presence of love. People soften and practically begin purring like kittens when they are acknowledged and praised.

But the ego believes that attack is what motivates people to do their best. Threatening, withholding, bargaining and making deals, whining, manipulating, micro-managing, self-pitying, withdrawing, sabotaging, disapproving, shaming, guilting, pleading, punishing . . . these are but some of the exhausting techniques that the ego uses as solutions to relationship problems.

Yet in the end, only love heals. This is why the ego fears it so. To the ego, love is weakness. The ego tells you that if you radically love, you are merely a doormat to be taken advantage of because love is the province of weaklings and victims. This is the exact opposite of Truth. ONLY love heals.

If you will begin to practice radical love and praise with ALL the people around you, you may begin to experience an ease and a joy in your relationships that you have only seen on some of your old 1950's TV series. It will rock your world and change reality as you now know it. And the more you practice it, the more you will activate and attract this Love Principle in all aspects of your life. And when you don't, you will FEEL the contrast within yourself and realize that ALL the love and praise you scatter about your world is FIRST coming through YOU. All that you give is given to yourself first.

91

Paying Up Front

> "Everyone you offer healing to returns it. Everyone you attack keeps it and cherishes it by holding it against you. Whether he does this or not will make no difference; you will think he does. It is impossible to offer what you do not want without this penalty. **The cost of giving is receiving.** Either it is a penalty from which you suffer, or the happy purchase of a treasure to hold dear."
>
> A Course In Miracles

You may not realize it, and few do, but you are paying up front for everything you experience either through your direct action or through what you are holding in your consciousness. Therefore it is far better to do this consciously and deliberately than lazily through lack of awareness and understanding. Cause creates an effect in one way or another, though they may not always be physically manifested. You PAY attention—you PAY in one kind of energy or another, and you then GET whatever you have paid for whether you want it or not.

There is another way. There is the way of peace and effortless accomplishment. This has to do with GIVING AND RECEIVING instead of paying and getting. It is as simple and easy as breathing in and breathing out. Unfortunately in that analogy many of you are more comfortable with one or the other. You think it is far nobler to exhale than to inhale so you feel guilty about inhaling. You think of yourself as an "exhaler" and so you expel your breath as if you are trying to get rid of it. Or you greedily suck in as much air as possibly trying to hoard it as if the space will soon run out of oxygen. All your plans are about getting more oxygen and keeping hold of it. Of course this analogy seems insane. And it is insane. And it is quite true for most humans.

When you stop thinking of paying and getting and instead shift to giving and receiving, you will begin to understand that everything you give is given to yourself. When you drop your bargaining-bartering mentality, you will find an easy relaxed attitude toward the flow of all energies in your world. Giving becomes the happy purchase of a treasure to hold dear—but the holding is not a gripping of the hands. Instead, you learn to hold ALL lightly in your heart—neither trying to keep nor to get rid of. You can drop the habit of paying up front and you become extremely generous while at the same time becoming a very gracious receiver. There is no need to hoard or keep records of who gave what to whom and when. You live in the awareness that the Universal Accounts balance themselves without your interference.

Think more in terms of generously giving—to your body, to your job, to your relationships, to your world, to your life. Never give out any energy you yourself would not want to experience. And then simply be open to graciously receive because if you do not block it, all the energies you give out will always return to you. The more tense you are, the less open to receive you are. We begin RIGHT NOW. Today is a day of breakthrough for you dear miracle worker. DO NOT GET EXCITED by this news but rather cultivate an attitude of humble calm delight. The tide of your good is starting to come in today. Savor and enjoy the experience in a normal natural way because that is exactly what it is—normal and natural.

92

There Is Nothing Wrong With You

"God does not change His Mind about you, for He is not uncertain of Himself. And what He knows can be known, because He does not know it only for Himself. He created you for Himself, but He gave you the power to create for yourself so you would be like Him. That is why your mind is holy."

A Course In Miracles

What the world thinks of you is none of your business. Be concerned only with what God thinks of you for God's opinion never varies in the slightest. Even your own evaluation of yourself changes constantly and is not to be counted on. God KNOWS you, for you are His creation and He is well pleased with what He has made.

Remember that your behavior is determined by your self-perception. You ACT like whoever you believe yourself to be at the moment. This is why you do the things you do. It is also why at times you do the things you do NOT want to do. Without a completely stable self-perception your behavior cannot be completely consistent either.

To have a stable self-perception you must begin to see yourself through the eyes of Source. Nothing you do or do not do changes God's evaluation of you, which is that you are totally precious, lovable and loving. Nothing you do can change God's total love for you nor change Heaven's evaluation of you. Your mistakes are merely seen as a call for love and correction, not for contempt and punishment. Keep in mind that a parent does not despise the baby for falling down when learning to walk. Even the baby born without legs is celebrated and adored by a sane parent and God is THE totally sane parent of all Creation.

Therefore, begin today to accept God's evaluation of you as your own as well. STOP identifying yourself by your mistakes and errors. Stop identifying yourself by your pathology and diagnoses, or by your past history and character "defects." Do not insult your Maker by calling yourself anything less than totally worthy and miraculous. THERE IS NOTHING WRONG WITH YOU.

Tell yourself frequently, *"There is nothing wrong with me. I deserve to live and be happy today for God made me exactly as I am, and as I am not. I accept God's opinion of me as the only legitimate one worth considering and today **I agree with God** that I am perfectly normal in my own unique way. And since God is FOR me, nothing against me has any power to affect me at all. I am standing in the Light and Love of God today. I am his beloved child and I live in His perfect Grace today. I expect today to unfold in joyous and miraculous ways as I go forth seeing only the best in myself and the best in all those* *who cross my path. We are all sisters and brothers—the adored children of an infinitely loving Mother-Father God. I will form no opinion of anyone I see today no matter how they act or what they say for I know that the only opinion that matters is God's and so I will not criticize what God has made. We are all released together today to celebrate the great diversity of the manifested world Mind has made. I am safe. I am whole. I am happy for I am loved by God and there is nothing wrong with me."*

93

You Are Doing A Great Job!

"Yet whether or not you recognize it now, you have agreed to cooperate in the effort to become both harmless and helpful, attributes that must go together. Your attitudes even toward this are necessarily conflicted, because all attitudes are ego-based. This will not last. Be patient a while and remember that the outcome is as certain as God."

A Course In Miracles

Each moment is a choice between a grievance or a miracle, fear or love, torment or peace. You are becoming much more aware and adept at making the better choice! We are here to celebrate you today! Your willingness is gradually yet continually decreasing your inner conflicts, and this always makes you more accessible to the Atonement Principle. You are expressing love and kindness more freely in the ways that are uniquely yours.

You are learning to admit your mistakes more quickly and to turn to Us to guide you back on course again. Because of this, you are making fewer mistakes in general and are finding greater equanimity in your daily walk. You are far less reactive than you once were. You are also learning to lighten up with laughter and to enjoy the process more. Remember that when you get very serious, you are again attached to the nightmare and have momentarily forgotten the Truth.

Remember too that "retrogression is temporary" so that you do not make such a big deal out of your own errors and what you see as setbacks or delays. When you feel guilty because of your errors, you will also project guilt and shame onto others for their errors. This is the opposite of helpful. As long as you are in a body you will make mistakes and be learning. Do not be hard on yourself, but DO maintain your vigilance in surrendering all errors to the Holy Spirit for gentle Correction.

As you must know by now, We are using you more and more to be truly Helpful. We are so grateful to you for accepting your part in the return to sanity. You make Us smile. We love you so much. Allow Us to celebrate you today. We are ready to offer you a promotion now. And the Kingdom is the opposite of the ego realm. In the ego kingdom, each promotion brings more stress, worry, responsibility, seriousness, fear and ego attachments. In the Kingdom, each promotion brings more fun, laughter, joy, effortlessness, play and release from fear. Remember, We need HAPPY teachers in order to awaken others. If you are willing, today We are promoting you to a new level of Happy Teacher.

94

The Insane Pursuit of Specialness

"Pursuit of specialness is always at the cost of peace."
A Course In Miracles

"Special" is nothing more than a code word for "tormented." The ego is fanatical in its relentless pursuit of specialness, which is surprising when you look around and see the depressed state of those who have a sense of being special. To FEEL special is to feel separate. Special is THE defining characteristic of separation whether one is special in a "better than others" version or a "worse than others" version. And separation is what causes ALL depression, fear, anxiety and LONELINESS. Those who feel special are deeply painfully lonely above all else. Being special is the booby prize of the ego world.

Nothing is more insulting to the ego mind than to be called average or ordinary. Yet average and ordinary is THE most excellent thing anyone can be—it is THE state of remaining as God created you. The rose, the sunrise, the rainbow, the butterfly . . . these are all average and ordinary expressions of the One Life. Unique is different than special. All are unique and yet all are ordinary, not special. No two snowflakes are exactly alike and yet they are all average ordinary snowflakes. There is no competition or pursuit of excellence in snow flaking.

The ego teaches you that your specialness will bring you the love that you seek. The EXACT OPPOSITE is true. Specialness brings the deepest loneliness humans ever experience. Specialness is exclusion. Many pursue specialness as a way to protect themselves from the hurts of a long gone past. They try to become so special that they can never be hurt again. They strive for a personal "excellence" which will dissolve all their feelings of worthlessness and isolation. But what specialness does is build a cement wall around those dark feelings, locking them in with their own inner-bully and tormentor.

Those who embrace both their uniqueness along with their average ordinary nature tend to live joyous lives free of competition and comparison. They feel no need to BE SOMEBODY or to ACHIEVE something great in order to be noticed or set apart from others. It's not about who the world calls special—it is who FEELS special. There are people in your culture who are "stars" who feel perfectly ordinary and human, and others living in total obscurity who FEEL they are extraordinary and set apart from other mere mortals. This is insanity and it is a kind of mental cancer that eats away at the host.

Have you not noticed the trajectory of so many of your fellow humans path to specialness? There is the rise above the crowd followed by the inevitable breakdown and descent into one form of madness or another, whether mild or extreme in nature. And your world has become obsessed with specialness to an alarming degree. This correlates with the rise in anxiety and depression disorders. They go together. Have you also not noticed how many average ordinary people are happily going about their lives while uplifting the vibration of the entire planet in their own ordinary yet unique ways? Many of your lives have been positively changed by a stranger earning minimum wage standing behind a counter, or by a harried schoolteacher who made one innocent encouraging sentence to you 30 years ago, or by a "mutt" with no pedigree from the animal shelter. Ordinary people working together built the pyramids.

Every being is gifted by God. This is part of your uniqueness and it is to be honored and cultivated. Each being is a thread in the multi-colored Master Tapestry which makes up the whole of Creation. No thread is more special than any other yet each one is necessary and has an important function in the Whole. So though you may have some amazing special talents and abilities, they are not who or what you are. They are gifts of God, given to be used to joyfully Help summon the Light into the dark corners of your world. Embrace them, enjoy them, share them, honor them and do not let them define you.

Right now, all across your world, on this very day, ordinary average people are falling in love, having their first baby, starting their new business, feeding someone hungry, bandaging the wound, driving the kids to school, inventing something which will help millions of people, helping the children cross the street, scratching the cat's ear, writing the song, doing the filing, soothing a friend. EVERY single one of those things is important to the Whole and though some of them require a unique talent, none is MORE important than any of the rest. Your peace today will not come from the separation of specialness—it will come from the union with Source as a part of the Masterpiece of Creation.

95

You Are Important and Needed Here

"You are indeed essential to God's plan. Without your joy, His joy is incomplete. Without your smile, the world cannot be saved. While you are sad, the light that God Himself appointed as the means to save the world is dim and lusterless, and no one laughs because all laughter can but echo yours."

A Course In Miracles

Your role in God's plan is essential. And your role is to allow yourself to be filled with the JOY of the love of God. That's all. You are sent as a happy ambassador into each segment and situation of your day in order to radiate JOY whether anyone chooses to accept it or not, whether anyone likes it or not.

It is not so much a "doing" but rather a state of being. There is no need to "cheer others up" or get them to see the good in life. Your energy does the work. It is not your job to convince anyone of anything, to get them to change their ways, to convert them but merely to **accept them as they are while you maintain your state of JOY in their presence**. You do not need for them to approve of you, to "get" you, to understand you, to agree with you, to tolerate you, or even to leave you be—your role is to maintain your own JOY no matter what.

YES, We understand how difficult you find that at times— that's why it's called a course in MIRACLES and not a course in manipulation and defensiveness. Ultimately this is what all these lessons have been about—maintaining your own JOY no matter what—under any and all circumstances. What We've been training you for from the very start is how to discipline your mind to FOCUS on the thoughts that cultivate JOY and inner peace. This is what our boot camp is all about; training you to take your extremely essential role in the Great Campaign of returning the mind's of the children of God back to sanity, JOY and inner peace. This is not a path of sad sacrifice and martyrdom. We require HAPPY teachers. And to teach is to demonstrate.

Just how happy and joyful are you willing to be? Ask yourself this daily. It is not a silly question. It deserves and requires some contemplation and reflection. In the contemplation of it you may begin to see how much loyalty you still have to the ego and it's body identification thought system. This awareness allows you to make a better choice. You merely are choosing between being host to God, or hostage to the ego.

You ARE important. We LOVE you. There is much We have to accomplish through you and We accomplish most efficiently and effortlessly through you when you are marinating in the JOY of God's Presence.

96

People Who Need People

"The plan is not of you, nor need you be concerned with anything except the part that has been given you to learn. For He Who knows the rest will see to it without your help. But think not that He does not need your part to help Him with the rest. For in your part lies all of it, without which is no part complete, nor is the whole completed without your part. The ark of peace is entered two by two, yet the beginning of another world goes with them. Each holy relationship must enter here, to learn its special function in the Holy Spirit's plan, now that it shares His purpose."

A Course In Miracles

Independence is an ego myth. It does not exist anywhere in all of eternity. No one and nothing can nor does stand alone. When the Course reminds you that "the lonely journey fails" take this to heart. Of yourself you cannot survive nor thrive in any way. You already depend on thousands, and for some of you even millions, of people every single day. To even buy a loaf of bread or to make a bank deposit is an enormous collaborative venture involving the hands and intentions of many many people you will never know. Within the world illusion, even your lungs are dependent on the plant life to give you what you need to physically maintain "life" in the body.

Those who believe they are independent and self-sufficient do not realize how EXTREMELY dependent they are on others. This dependence is GOOD news and to be embraced. It means that you are in a constant state of miracle potentiality. Miracles have nothing to do with God at all. Revelation is what happens between God and His children, but miracles are what happen between the Sons and Daughters of God. And miracles cannot occur without a softening of the heart and the head. You cannot maintain your guard and at the same time allow another person into your heart. Fear of being hurt blocks love and it STOPS miracles from occurring.

Many of you are afraid that any dependence on another would make you weak, unlovable, unattractive. But again, your babies and pets have no shame at all about their dependence on you and yet your love for them soars. The simple fact is, humans LIKE to feel needed when it is done in a healthy balanced way. Get in the habit of ASKING people for help in a balanced healthy way. And set people free to say yes or no with no hard feelings. Your job is to ask, allow and receive but not to demand. Ask warmly and boldly—no whining, no pleading, no making deals or negotiating. Just stand still and be soft and open as you ASK for whatever help you feel you need. It is as much a gift to the one being asked as it is to you. People WANT to contribute to you in balanced healthy ways but you must take the risk of letting down your shield. With these kinds of "risks" come big rewards.

Each day you have many chances to feel the tremendous love of the Holy Relationship reverberating through you. Even the Lone Ranger had a trusty scout Tonto. You are not alone. No one is alone.

97

Feed the Champion

"What fear would feed upon, love overlooks. What fear demands, love cannot even see."

A Course In Miracles

Feeding the champion. It is good for you to stop and acknowledge just how far you have come in these lessons by feeding your inner champion. You are continually learning not to feed the ego, which is the inner bully, and have instead begun the excellent habit of feeding your true Self, the champion within you. What is actually happening in this process is that you are changing and refining your appetites.

However, it will do little good if you think of these spiritual boot camps as something you do for a while to clean up your vibration and then you just go right back to your old ways as soon as it is over. This would be like saying, *"Well, I brushed my teeth so thoroughly and completely this morning that I don't think I will ever need to do it again!"* Backsliding can happen very quickly without proper attention and diligence.

The purpose of these boot camps is to instill new habits which create an energetic momentum that will continue to reap rewards and benefits for as long as you continue putting energy into it each day—even long after the boot camp is completed. The difference is that when you begin a new way of thinking and living it takes a much greater effort because you are changing the direction of the inertia. You'd been going in one direction and are now turning around to go in the opposite direction. Now that you've been going in this new direction for some time, it takes much less energy to continue going forward.

When you were being taught to brush your teeth as a small child, perhaps you had to be nagged by your parents to do it. It took a lot of energy to ingrain the habit. It was a decision that you had to be endlessly reminded of making each day. But by now, there is no decision to make. You don't DECIDE whether you will brush your teeth each day. You just do it because it's a habit. Thinking is a habit too. Your thoughts are mental habit patterns which you learned—and you can and are learning new ones. Many of them have already started to take root in you and to bear good fruit.

BUT DO NOT GET LAZY AND SLOPPY about this or you may find that you have once again started feeding those old ego fear-driven thoughts and concepts. Some time each and every day must be spent feeding and nourishing the champion within. A champion requires good quality nutrition in order to meet each challenge of the day and even in order to simply rest in JOY.

So the question each day becomes, *"What am I feeding the Champion today?"*

98

Don't Pick It Up!

"The past is the ego's chief learning device, for it is in the past that you learned to define your own needs and acquired methods for meeting them on your own terms."

A Course In Miracles

The obsession with the past is what keeps creating a present and future just like the past—not in form, but in feeling. As you continue to tell the story of being abandoned 30 years ago, you will FEEL abandoned in the present even though you may be surrounded by loved ones. As you tell the story of the loss of love 20 years ago, you will fail to FEEL the love which is here and now. Even if you keep FOCUSING on how much better the past was, you are basically invalidating today and wasting your now.

Anything from your past which did not teach you to be a happier and more loving person TODAY is nothing more than a lie, a distortion of the ego thought system. Let it go by not picking it up to begin with. When you ask "but HOW do I let this go?" you are asking the wrong question. The question is not how to let it go for letting go is not a doing at all—it is a NOT doing. HOLDING ON IS A DOING. Picking something up is a doing. Letting go is when you simply relax and STOP doing. In the relaxing, it falls from your hands.

So instead, begin noticing WHEN and HOW you pick up suffering, longing, sadness, grief, depression, anxiety, anger, and any stories which disturb you. Begin to notice the first thought so that you can make a better choice. Begin to notice when you are picking up an old story from the past instead of focusing on your NOW. You can most effectively STOP picking up your suffering by picking up something else instead, for you cannot hold two opposing thoughts at the same time. You may go back and forth between the two many times a day, but you cannot hold them both in mind at the same time.

Remember that it is progress, not perfection. You are creating new habits of thought so give yourself time and patience, but do not give up. Keep going. The more you practice, the easier it gets. And eventually you will notice that you are picking up joy, peace, love and harmony more than anything else. Penguin steps.

99

The Turnaround Point

"As the course emphasizes, you are not free to choose the curriculum, or even the form in which you will learn it. You are free, however, to decide when you want to learn it. And as you accept it, it is already learned."

A Course In Miracles

Everyone has a turnaround point. It is the place where you tend to drop the class because it has gotten too uncomfortable and you just don't want to go on. Yet there is no graduation without completion of the class. This world is not merely an illusion, it is also a school and you **will** learn whatever you came to learn, whether in this lifetime or in the next or the next or the next. Why not press on and complete the curriculum now?

It's as if you keep signing up for the class and then dropping it as soon as you have an issue with the teacher or the other students. So you keep signing up with cuter teachers in prettier classrooms not realizing that the curriculum is EXACTLY the same every single time. In your life experience this feels like getting to the same place over and over again and then not progressing to the next level. It's because you keep turning around and going back to your comfort zone and waiting for a new semester to begin.

You must KNOW that you CAN complete this class! You must SAY this to yourself frequently and you must change your attitude about the class and the teachers. As you release your resistance to the curriculum and the teachers, you will find that things progress MUCH more smoothly and joyfully. Make peace with the teachers and the curriculum. Encourage yourself and REMEMBER that you are not alone. We are here to Help you with your studies. ASK Us for Help in GENTLY pressing on through. We have Helped billions of beings go through EXACTLY what you are going through. We have your back. You can do this. You can do this. You can do this.

100

No Accidents

"Therefore the plan includes very specific contacts to be made for each teacher of God. There are no accidents in salvation. Those who are to meet will meet, because together they have the potential for a holy relationship. They are ready for each other."

A Course In Miracles

This is another reason why you can call off the search. You will meet whomever you are assigned to meet the moment you are ready for each other whether this means a friend, an employer, a co-worker or business contact, your son or daughter, a mate . . . anyone and everyone. And you will NOT meet whomever you are not assigned to meet no matter how hard you struggle and strive. BE GLAD! You may now relax, breathe easy and allow yourself to BE yourself exactly as you are. If there are changes that need to be made in you, the Holy Spirit will Help to make those positive changes to the extent that you allow.

Relax today and go about your business knowing that the more you trust in God, the easier the day will go. Rest in the awareness that no part of the plan for your ultimate joy has been left out. Stop looking at your watch and calendar! Stop reminding the Universe how long you've been waiting. THAT is what keep you from being ready and delays each appointed meeting. Impatience is a sign that you are NOT ready yet—that your self-will has still not been brought under the control of your Higher Self.

True relaxing does not make you unconscious; it makes you calmly present and alert. You think of relaxation and deep slumber when in reality, deep relaxation is a heightened awareness of NOW without any clinging to the past or anticipation of the future other than to watch where you are going.

Let go, relax and trust that God is here now, that there is a Divine Plan for your happiness. Go inside and LISTEN, We have things to tell you today. Please, spend some time with Us listening as We soothe and uplift you. Do not avoid Us because you are "too busy" or distracted. We can save you a lot of time and wasted energy. We are the Messengers of God, sent to Help and Guide you. Let Us do our job.

101

And So We Say Amen

"This course is a beginning, not an end. Your Friend goes with you. You are not alone. No one who calls on Him can call in vain. Whatever troubles you, be certain that He has the answer, and will gladly give it to you, if you simply turn to Him and ask it of Him."

A Course In Miracles

Many times on this journey We have reminded you of this Truth; that "you are not alone." We are as near as your breath, closer than your hands and feet. Your Eternal Friend will never leave you comfortless nor without direction. And though the lessons never end, more and more you are becoming a joyful learner because you are trusting less in your own strength as you rely on the strength of your Friend Who lives within.

The end of one journey is the start of yet another. Each journey becomes lighter and more enjoyable as you practice walking in joy and in love. This becomes the focus of teaching and learning now; sharing the peace and joy of God without struggle and strain, giving and receiving rather than paying and getting, praising rather than complaining, trusting instead of worrying, sharing instead of hoarding, forgiving instead of attacking. We will Help you every step of the way and We are greatly impressed with your progress and willingness. We thank you for doing what you came here to do. We thank you for your continued willingness and dedication. We thank you for listening, learning and doing.

And this is not the end, but rather a happier beginning of an even more joyful journey forward in the Light.

About the Author

Jacob Glass is an author and spiritual teacher who lectures monthly in San Diego, Los Angeles, Palm Springs and Santa Barbara. For dates, locations and other information on his CD's, mp3's, blogs and spiritual resources, please see his website: www.jacobglass.com

Suggested Reading

A Return to Love by Marianne Williamson
Battlefield of the Mind by Joyce Meyer
A Course in Miracles by the Foundation for Inner Peace
The Neville Reader by Neville Goddard
Living by Grace by Joel Goldsmith
Question Your Thinking, Change The World by Byron Katie

CPSIA information can be obtained at www.ICGtesting.com
Printed in the USA
LVOW100432060712

288925LV00003B/1/P